OLD BRIZE N

10
BRIZE
NORTON
OXON

OLD BRIZE NORTON

Through the eyes of two young girls

**Kathy Timms
and
Clare Hicks**

BOOKMARQUE
PUBLISHING

First published December 2002

© Kathy Timms and Clare Hicks

The authors assert their moral rights

British Library Cataloguing in Publication Data

A catalogue record for this book is available from the British Library

ISBN 1870519-68-X

Frontispiece:
Brize Norton School and Church circa the nineteen-twenties.

Typeset in 11 on 14pt Palatino
Typesetting, design and origination by Bookmarque
Published by Bookmarque Publishing
Printed and bound by Antony Rowe Ltd

Contents

To the children of
Brize Norton School
in the Golden Jubilee Year of
Queen Elizabeth the Second
2002

Opposite page:
Kathy (on the right) with her sister, Muriel, photographed in 1924.

Below:
Clare (on the right) with her sister, Marie, photographed in 1924.

Introduction and Acknowledgements

The idea to write this book came to us when we both realised that our childhood had been something rather special. We lived all our school years before the aerodrome came and changed Brize Norton from its position as a quiet Cotswold village to a place of great importance, especially during the Second World War, and as a consequence it became known worldwide.

This book is written for those who have never experienced the self-contained place that Brize Norton once was, and for those who never knew the people who made it what it was.

We are still immensely proud of our village and how it has coped with all the changes, and yes, we think it is still a most marvellous place to live!

We would like to offer our grateful thanks to all those kind people from whom we have gleaned information relevant to the characters in this book, and also to those who entrusted us with their family photographs. To mention but a few: Mr Bill Upstone, Miss Betty Giles, Sydney Timms, and John Cambray for his efforts to get us a picture of the Old Forge, to Eva and Lucy (Field) for the information on Moat Farm and the Methodist Chapel, to our families, especially Fred (Clare's husband) who gave his time when we needed it, and also to Mrs Barbara Studwell for kindly editing our manuscript.

We would also like to extend our thanks to Nigel Fisher for the photograph on the back cover.

Finally, we are very much indebted to Tom Worley for his encouragement and enthusiasm, without which the book would never have got off the ground, and to John Rose for publishing the result.

Kathy Timms and Clare Hicks
Brize Norton
Oxfordshire

Chapter 1

Railway Station End

Seventy-seven years ago two young girls, Clare and Kathy, started school in the village of Brize Norton in Oxfordshire, (probably on the same day). Ever since they have been friends. Mostly they would meet at school because they lived nearly a mile apart. Much of what they learnt sunk in, and they also learnt to love the countryside and the village.

The village boundary on the east and south side was Norton Ditch, clearly marked on the village map. Kathy lived just inside that boundary on the south side, the other side of it was in Bampton parish. Also just inside that boundary was Bampton railway station, a branch line from Fairford to Oxford—it was a busy place in the 1920s carrying both passengers and goods.

The first train in the morning arrived at 7.30 a.m. and it was called the milk train. There were four stations before Bampton: Fairford, Lechlade, Kelmscot and Langford, and Alvescot; milk was collected from these four stations and then loaded into the goods waggons. This train took passengers as well, primarily business people who were going either to Oxford or to Witney.

The next train down from Oxford at 8.30 a.m. brought the morning papers. These were sorted in the waiting room on a large square table by Mr Matthews from Carterton whose business it was. Mr Matthews then packed them on to the back of his bicycle and delivered them to the top end of Brize Norton village, and from there on to Carterton. The lower end of the village had their papers delivered by a young lad named Frank Faulkner and you could hear him coming as he was always whistling and had a smile and words for everyone.

Back at the station the engine was shunted into a siding ready to propel the train from the back; the Witney Grammar School children were waiting for it, ten or twelve of them, and Kathy's

9

sister was among them—most had passed their Eleven-plus examination, which entitled them to this honour.

Around the station there were lovely coloured posters of places that could be reached by rail; Skegness, Bournemouth, Weymouth, and even Wales and Scotland, and there was a tempting Nestlés chocolate machine where one could get a bar for tuppence (2d or in today's money just 0.83 of one pence!) that you could eat in one mouthful.

The railway line was a real treat to wander along. Here grew all the wild flowers that one could think of—Clare especially liked the harebell. The cowslips grew in big clumps, so they were fine too, and then there were the moon daisies, buttercups and wild pansies, and here and there were quaker grasses.

Close to the line was the fox cover—a mass of golden gorse in midsummer—and had a strong smell of foxes. The huntsmen often turned a fox out of here, and in spite of its many winding pathways we did not venture in very far because the scrub scratched our arms too much, but sometimes we would actually see a vixen with her cubs playing in the sunshine, jumping over one another, and having a good time—this was a sight not to be missed! Later in the year mushrooms popped up all over the place, and we took a bucket to put them in. Field mushrooms are far superior to the ones bought in the supermarket—and how we gorged ourselves, often with dire consequences!

We must move on from the railway line, although it would be nice to linger and listen to the skylarks, singing high up in the sky, but there would be a puff of white smoke emerging under Lew bridge—a train was coming and we must get to safety, and just savour the nostalgic smell of the steam on the hot coals.

There were other places to visit, but not all on the same day. Nesbits Copse at Lower Haddon Farm, with a mass of primroses to see. We took balls of odd wool to tie them into bunches and Kathy and her sister Muriel had little bridesmaid's baskets made of cane to collect them in.

It was a beautiful sight to see those primroses, and we would move quickly from clump to clump looking for the finest flowers (we did not pick the wild anemones because they would fade before we got back home). The rooks were cawing up in the tall elm trees as it was nesting time, and twigs were being fitted into the nests that would soon hold the young.

The children down the lane, who Kathy and her sister went with, were the farm-workers' children; Eddy, Cyril, Audrey and Betty Drinkwater, together with the Hicks twins, Delphine and Stella (who our schoolmaster unkindly referred to them both as Delphinium and Nasturtium!) They all lived down Diddly Corner, as it was known locally, and the boys on the look out for bird's nests were reminded that the birds would desert if they were touched.

Before they went home Kathy and her sister would go with these children to an old barn, it clearly had been a church at some time because it had a big cross on the side and arched windows. Something always held Kathy back—she felt it was a sacred place and she could not romp about on the hay with the rest, fearing that she would be damned for ever if she joined in; this was probably because she attended the strict Baptist church at Alvescot each Sunday, so she was glad to creep away.

Clare went to the old barn too, with her sister Marie. People would have to be aged well over seventy now to remember it, because it was pulled down to make way for the Brize Norton aerodrome in the early 1930s.

In an old book by W. J. Monk, he describes the old church barn as part of the parish of Bampton, where there was an old house called Little Haddon, and there in this old house, so tradition says, the Roman Catholic plot was hatched, in the early days of Queen Elizabeth I, which created such a sensation. It also asserted that Edward Campion, the great revolutionist, slept there on the night before he was arrested for High Treason. The church barn is built in cruciform and very frequently with ecclesiastical structures. There are other features which denote that it was used as a private chapel for those of the Catholic faith, and it may have continued secretly after the reformation, when it was illegal to build chapels.

11

THE OLD BARN AT LITTLE HADDON

Not very far from the primrose copse was another strange place, 'Pond Gardens', this was another wooded area with several deep ponds in it but whether it was man-made or a natural feature is uncertain. In there grew the fritillary, a poisonous but protected plant, with bell-shaped flowers. It is purple-brown with a mottled chessboard pattern—we called them snake flowers, and never picked them. We were also told that there actually were snakes in this strange place, and one was seen in the adjoining field owned by Kathy's father.

In those idyllic days of the nineteen-twenties, there was little for parents to worry about regarding just where their children were—it was felt quite safe for the children to wander in the countryside. A few gypsies were about, in caravans drawn by piebald ponies, with a few lurcher dogs tied to the van, but they were harmless.

There was an old woman from Bampton who would take her pram into the villages, going from door to door, with her big basket which contained some tatty lace. People would buy a yard or so just to be rid of her, and sometimes, if you had not bought from her, she needed watching—a few onions here or a carrot or two would get into her basket in the twinkling of an eye!

Then there was the old tramp by the name of 'Itchy Coo'. He would frighten children and torment isolated houses for a bit of food. He often did this at Kathy's home, and when no-one answered the door he could be a real nuisance especially at a place like Colebrook Villa, which was a mile out of the village, but he only appeared once or twice a year, thank goodness!

It's a mile from the bottom of the Station Hill to the church—at one time there had been a milestone there, but it was moved to make an entrance to the RAF Station—however, the one by the church is still there, let into the wall by the cemetery.

On our way to the village from the railway station, the first buildings we come to, on the left, were at Marsh Haddon Farm and at that time it belonged to James Hoskins. He was what we called a gentleman farmer, and he owned a nice big farm and farmhouse set about with tidy farm buildings. The family did not mix much with the village people, although once a year the Women's Institute were invited down to a garden party during the summer. Belonging to the farm were a row of cottages, each one could only be reached by crossing the wide stream that came all the way down from the village, so each had a bridge and a little picket gate. The flower gardens for the cottages were at the front making a very pretty picture in the summer time. Boys loved to try to catch the trout that were in the stream.

Before the Hoskins there were the Morleys and they were about the last to use the old steam engines on the farm. One of these engines was still about then and could be seen being driven up and down the village by 'Tanky' Mills. He would give children a ride—it was fascinating to see him turning the wheel about. He was always polishing the engine and keeping the brass shining.

The furthest cottages were two made into one, that the Lohmann's lived in. Mr Lohmann was killed in the First World War, leaving Mrs Lohmann to bring up her son, Maurice, and daughter, Gweneth (Gwen). She was very small in stature, but she was intelligent and had a nice singing voice, and she would sing at the village concerts. Maurice was a quiet man, a good tennis player, and he also kept poultry from which he made a living. Gwen could often be seen carrying her little cane basket of eggs up into the village.

In the same field there was a path leading to the bluebell

copse. This was a lovely place with tall elm trees and bluebells covering all the ground. We gathered as many as we could carry, but this was made difficult because the stems were long and slimy, so we usually left a trail of bluebells behind us!

Marsh Haddon Farm, the cottages, the stream with trout in, and the bluebell wood all disappeared to make way for the aerodrome, but a few people still have their memories of it.

Next we pass the plantation, which was another wooded area. Kath never went into it thinking it a bit spooky, but Clare used to go boldly in with her older sister, Marie. There they found a walnut tree, that may have been the attraction, as not many people knew about it!

Just past the plantation (which is still there today) was a small area called 'Gravel Pits', part of it was made into small allotment which belonged to the council. The only people who used it were Min Archer and her sister Nelly, and they made the journey backwards and forwards with Min pushing the wheel-

Little Gwen Lohmann with Bill Upstone.

Brize Norton and Bampton Railway Station circa 1930s.

barrow. Both were well-known characters in the village, who loved a bit of gossip but were always ready to help anyone in trouble. Many years ago it was a natural drainage place for surface water for the village. Later the village sewerage was piped down there and was transferred to the water board. A bit further up on the left-hand side of the road were two very tall elm trees, big in girth, and by their position they appeared to be the entrance to the village. Friends would go for a walk only as far as the tall trees. They were eventually felled for being unsafe.

The road through the village was the usual tarmac and chippings. Every few years this was resurfaced—another occurrence that fascinated the children. It would begin with two or three men brushing the road in order to get a good dust free surface, then it would have hot tar spread again with brooms to cover the surface. Next came a wheelbarrow full of chippings to cover the tar, followed by the big steam roller used to bed-in the chippings—backwards and forwards it would go. How we savoured the smell of that tar. But we were careful "Not to get any on your clothes!" [mothers' words]. That was it for another few years.

In those days we had a roadman, Mr Drinkwater, who, as well as keeping the roads and pathways clear in the village, also kept the path all the way down to the station clear, but sadly he died suddenly on the side of the road. He was replaced much later by Mr Fitchett who lived outside the village, on the Burford road.

Clare recalls a Mr Jackson who had a carrier's business delivering goods from Carterton to Bampton Station. On his return to Carterton he took bags of coal for his customers—he drove a mule and they do say 'stubborn as a mule' and this mule was daddy of them all. Just before he started climbing Station Hill, the mule would drop down, sometimes for the whole day! Mr Jackson would whip him, rant and rave, and throw his arms about, but the mule would not budge! The shout would echo through the village "Jackson's mule is down." Kathy, not knowing the full story thought Jackson was a cruel madman, always shouting and thrashing his mule—but maybe this was the only way to keep his awkward beast going?

An exciting feature of summer was the ice cream man who came with his little cart from Faringdon. He was an Italian gentleman, and the little 'cart' was pulled by a very quiet pony. The cart was Italian in style with white frills along the roof, the Italian gent (his name was Joe Giannadrea) wore white clothes and a straw hat with coloured ribbons attached. His ice cream was glorious, or so it seemed to us children. Another ice cream vendor would come up the road from Bampton—he rode a bicycle with a deep box in front like a tradesman's bicycle. His 'Elderaldo' ice cream was nothing like Joe Giannadrea's, very disappointing, and a small wrapped bar would cost tuppence.

The village seemed to be well supplied by tradesmen—a Mr Walker (known as 'Hog Pudding Walker') came regularly from Witney by bicycle. On the front of this was a very large basket carrying 'Hogs Puddings', believed to be made from barley meal and pork, with seasoning. Shaped like sausages, and tied with loops, and very beautifully made, were carefully presented in this big basket covered with a pristine white cloth.

Mrs Bert Timms, Landlady at *The Carpenters Arms* (known locally as the 'Axe'), used to make wonderful faggots after a pig killing—local people would 'knock at the back door' taking with them a big jug, and she would fill it with gravy and faggots for just a few pennies. This was a very cheap meal for the village people who had little access to a butcher's shop.

Chapter 2

The Entrance to the Village

On entering the village after the big trees, the first holding on the west side is Upper Haddon Farm, The farm house is a grade two listed building of the eighteenth century, with two storeys and an attic. It is a large house having five bedrooms, and on the ground floor a drawing room, a dining room, a living room and a large kitchen. There is also a dairy connected to the house.

There are a good number of fields on both sides of the road, reaching right back to the railway line.

Mr Thomas Pratt owned the farm in the 1920s—it was a dairy farm and there were also a few sheep. A number of employees were needed, such as cowmen and carters; tractors were not around then, so there were at least four working horses, all having names of course! Carts and waggons were used, and everything seemed to move at a much slower pace.

Mrs Ellen Pratt made dairy butter; she shaped it into oblongs, then put a criss-cross pattern on the top, and wrapped it in greaseproof paper and sold it mostly at the back door, although she did supply some to the local shops. She also sold skimmed milk, a by-product of the butter making, and local people would go to the back door with their cans and jugs: a quart would cost just a few pence and would be used for the everyday milk pudding.

Mr and Mrs Pratt travelled round the village in a rather high trap pulled by a pony. Their little dog, Brownie, always by their side. Mr Pratt died in 1932 aged fifty-nine, leaving Mrs Pratt to run the farm. This she did with the help of her brother-in-law, Mr Collett from Carterton, who was a farmer himself.

There were a good many cottages that went with the farm, so altogether Upper Haddon Farm took up a good chunk of the lower end of the village.

Bye's Cottage from a painting in 1952 and (below) Thatcher's place in the 1920s.

On Upper Haddon Farm was a place called the 'Cuckoo Pen', and in the hot summer holidays we were drawn to this place. It was about fourteen feet across, and maybe twenty feet long, and about three feet deep, and was part of a stream that came the whole length of the village. The stream could be traced back to Shilton, and was the same one that went past the cottages at Marsh Haddon.

Chapter 3

The Lower End

We rolled up and even took off some of our clothing, depending to who was about, and paddled in the water, trying to do a few breast strokes with one foot on the bottom! It was a bit murky if the cows had recently been in, and it had a bit of a smell too, but then one could not be fussy, the feel of the cool water on our hot little bodies could not have felt better if we were at some smart lido!

Following downstream to 'Cock Hatch' was another water attraction, what it meant or was for we had no idea, but it was the rush of the water through a narrower place, so deep too, one did not get too close, as with the sheep dipping place further on.

Just a little bit further away from the 'Cuckoo Pen' was another field that we had been told about, 'Cure All' it was called and at one time contained many herbs. Years ago women would go there if one of the family was sick, and they would know just the right herb to help them get better. It's a great pity that these old remedies have been forgotten. Also running along the the field was a pure stream, said to have properties

Upper Haddon Farm.

extremely good for the eyes, Clare said she and her sister often went there to bathe their eyes, with the firm belief that it would give them good eyesight.

Crossing the road from Upper Haddon Farm, we find the attractive Cotswold cottage *Bangalore*, where Mr Bert Bye, his wife Agnes, daughter Elsie, and sons Paul and John live.

The cottage was so called by Mr Bye as a reminder of his three years in Bangalore, southern India, during the 1914-1918 world war (previously it is believed that the cottage was called *Rose Cottage*). That dreadful war claimed many fathers and sons. And many suffered the after-effects from the war including Mr Bye.

'Jack the dog' was part of the Bye family, and was taught many a trick by Paul and John. The boys and their friends knew every inch of Upper Haddon Farm, where to catch a Bullhead, a small fish found in the ditches and considered a great prize, and also where the owls lay their eggs in the tumble-down barn halfway down the common, so they too enjoyed roaming the fields. Why it was called the common we do not know, for it was not considered a right of way by farmer Pratt, and the boys did act about like all boys do, but riding on the backs of sheep was not appreciated!

The common was where the cows were called in for milking. They took their leisurely preamble to the road, leaving impatient people waiting until the last awkward creature had lurched across the highway.

Both *Bangalore* (which had now become *Bye's Cottage*) and the next house, *Thatchers*, faced south with Upper Haddon just over the road. *Thatchers* got its name from the man who lived there, William Thatcher, who was a well-known character in the village. His transport was a horse and trap, and he quite often visited public houses, however, he was an amicable man who would always welcome a companion on his jaunts.

The story is told that his horse knew every pub in the district, and could be trusted to bring his master home when he became drowsy and even when his master was unable to hold the reins!

With *Thatchers* was a good sized garden, which had a well just in front of the living room window, (maybe that it why for a time it was called *Well Cottage*) and he also owned the sizeable adjoining field, that perhaps was how he made his living. His wife Isabel died in 1921, so maybe he drank to console himself? William Thatcher died in 1928 aged seventy-three, and later the house was sold to Mr Gale who lived there with his family of Emma, Lena and son Alex. Mr Gale kept cows in the field and started a small milk round in the village, which he did on his bicycle delivering from a large can fixed to his handle bars.

After the Gales left, a family named Cole moved in, they kept themselves to themselves very much, but the two sons made friends with the local children, sharing the Goldflake cigarettes that their parent bought in tins of fifties, with their friends, and starting many a young lad on the habit-forming pleasure of tobacco smoking.

Moving on, the next plot of land was Timms' Orchard, and children loved to get in there—they freely wandered about among the old fruit trees, so old that some were very nearly horizontal, and grew at all angles. There was a lovely meandering stream running through, with a few ducks quacking around, the cows made a mess where they paddled to get a drink.

The entrance was through two high corrugated doors, which showed signs of wear, and at one time had been painted black. Just inside the doors, which were usually half open, were two stone pig sties with sows and piglets.

About Easter time the stream would have frog-spawn in it, the children got so excited when they first noticed it, and jam jars were quickly fetched to gather a few slippy handfuls of it. This would be taken to school at the first opportunity and there it would be displayed on the window sill, along with the sticky buds of the horse chestnut tree, and it would be eagerly watched for the first movement of a wiggly tail of a tadpole. Sadly they never got beyond that stage and so no little frogs ever did appear. Well, perhaps next year?

Just across the road from Timms' orchard was an old cottage owned by Mr Billy Luckett, it was almost at the point of falling

Woodbine Cottage.

down. Half of the house was a stable and over the half open door of the stable a donkey looked out. Billy was an old man and he talked of soon going to live with his family. Mr Fred Timms wanted that cottage and so he paid a deposit on it, but no time was fixed for the takeover. Billy wanted to stay there for as long as he could manage, and at the same time Fred Timms was eager to do the move, so in the end he had to be given a bit of a push, and Billy moved on.

1933 Fred Timms took possession and started right away to build it up almost from the bottom, thus making a nice place for himself, his wife Amy and five sons. The family eventually moved in in 1934, taking their two dogs, Spot and Tiny, with them, and also a linnet in a cage. Fred designed a pretty garden in the front, where previously it had been just a yard. In the garden he put a proper sundial, and the local doctor showed him how to set it right for telling the time. They called the cottage *Sundial Cottage*, and it is still known by that name today.

Right in front of *Sundial Cottage* was a high wall, and the end of *Woodbine Cottage*. In the spring the air was filled with the beautiful fragrance of the honeysuckle on that wall from which it got it's name.

Timms' Orchard circa 1950s.

Woodbine Cottage belonged to Pratt's farm, and the end nearest the farmyard was an old fashioned barn, with a old look to it, and really quite attractive. It had a barn door and some upright stone mullions with no glass in them. The whole of *Woodbine Cottage* had a charm about it and obviously over the years it had been terribly neglected.

At that time a Mr Leonard Timms lived in the cottage, he was quite an old man, but he would still give a hand when needed for an hour or two on the farm. One day he was asked to help at

Sundial Cottage.

Woodbine Cottage, as painted by Kathy Timms.

haymaking time, and he replied: "I'll be along when I have drunk me tae!" He picked up the teapot and drank from the spout, then he was ready, he really was old and died in 1950 at the age of eighty-four, so he must have been born in 1866! Another old character gone...

Behind Billy Luckett's house was a small orchard belonging to Mr Pratt, and this separated it from *Jasmine Cottage* where Fred Timms and his family lived. Fred had inherited his father's builders and stone mason's business and he needed more room. Fred and his wife, Amy, had lived at Barrington previously, where four sons were born to them, another son, Arthur, was born after they moved to Brize Norton. Much, much later he would marry Kathy.

A great sadness came upon them in 1928 when their third son, Frederick, named after his father, tragically drowned at Buckland at a place called Tadpole. Although Frederick could swim he got trapped in the reeds. Amy never really got over it, he was only seventeen. But a few years later she began to look forward to moving to Billy's house, and it was from her little note book that Kathy found the entry in 1934: "moved in lock stock and barrel with two dogs and bird."

Jasmine Cottage looked over the local pub *The Carpenters Arms*, (the 'Axe'). In the summer the boys loved to see the men who got drunk. One time a customer was so dead drunk they picked him up, (he was only a small fellow) and put him on their father's hand cart, covered him with flowers and pushed him home.

Another amusing story was about the signalman from the station who would stay in the pub until he heard the hoot from the last train at ten-thirty, coming under Lew Bridge, this was to let him know that it was time to get on his bike and get to the station to put the signal down. It was known for the train to have to slow down and wait for him sometimes!

The 'Axe' was very popular with old and young men (not many women went into pubs in those days), sometimes a woman could be seen walking down with a jug in her hand to

The Carpenters Arms pub, better known by locals as the 'Axe'.

get some beer at the back door—it would be Mrs Timms who served her.

I know that when the Timms boys' cousin, Doris, came to stay for a holiday from Bristol, it was her delight to get on the piano in the pub. I know it was not what her parents had intended when they put her through an expensive course for the piano-forte, which allowed her to continue and to get letters after her name. This meant she could make a living out of giving lessons.

Doris was a young twenties' flapper, short skirt and doing the Can-Can, she loved to entertain belting out the tunes of the day: 'Bye-Bye Blackbird' was a favourite—the young men had never seen nor heard anything like it, they all fell in love with her, especially one! After Doris went home he rode his bike all the way to Bristol... Alas! Doris had a steady boyfriend whom she later married. (She would go on entertaining right up to the day she died, and was in great demand for the 'over-sixties clubs' even at the age of eighty.)

Things soon settled down, and Doris had promised to come back next year—which she did year after year—she loved Brize, it was where her mother had been born, when her grand-mother was postmistress.

Keeping on in front yard of the 'Axe', you would come to a secluded cottage, another *Rose Cottage*, here the Upstone family

Bill Upstone with horse.

26

A nice example of an Oxfordshire waggon.

lived. It belonged to Upper Haddon Farm. Mr and Mrs Upstone had children but how many there were we are not sure because some of the children died and they were a bit older than Clare and Kathy. Mr Upstone was known for his fine runner beans, which he said were planted in the same place, year after year— so much for the story that you must plant them in a different place each year! The family were devout Primitive Chapel people and would never miss a Sunday, and altogether were a very happy family in spite of the long lingering death of their daughter Kate.

There were other Upstone families in the village, but they did not appear connected in any way; perhaps if one could have traced the family tree we may have found that perhaps a long way back that they were distant cousins.

Passing on, the 'Axe' on our left, we go by the old skittle alley, where the game of Aunt Sally was played regularly until a few years ago. Apparently, Oxfordshire was one of a few counties that ever played the game, it could be played in teams, the aim being to see how many times Aunt Sally's head could be knocked off the three foot pole that it rested on. It was a great attraction, and it was also loaned out to local fêtes, some people became very good at it, and a lot of shouting went on.

The wall that continued on for about twenty feet after the skittle alley, rounding the corner in front of Knight's cottage, was a listed wall. What history was attached we do not know. It was and still is a well-built wall, and different to the Cotswold stone walls that surround the village. It stays very upright and it also looks as if at some time there could have been an opening in it.

The Knight family, who lived round the corner, had five children but they all moved away, with the exception of Christabel. She was named after Christabel Pankhurst—who with her mother, Emmeline Pankhurst, had founded and led the suffragette movement, The Women's Social and Political Union.

Christabel Knight married Percival, the oldest of the Timms boys. Mr Knight was chauffeur to Miss Cobb who lived at Bampton. Miss Cobb had one of the earliest limousines around, and Percival drove the car very sedately and proudly through Brize Norton, and was the envy of the young lads around.

Mrs Knight was mostly seen riding her 'sit-up-and-beg' bike to and from Bampton, her thin legs pushing the pedals round as fast as she could, and leaning over the bicycle basket as if to get to her destination even quicker! Gertrude Knight loved to be included in any family troubles around and would be the first to call if there was a death or illness in the family.

Gertrude collected contributions for the Oxford Infirmary, it was tuppence a week, this entitled one to the privilege of direct access to the hospital. A card was issued to each contributor, in which it was all recorded.

Christabel Knight and Percy Timms at their wedding in the mid 1930s.

28

After the Knight's house was a yard with high doors which were always kept padlocked—they were not far from the road. Behind those doors was a long track that led to *Paradise Cottage*. On the approach to the cottage were three open-fronted barns, and a delightful orchard, which were all on the right. This and a good sized field was all that was left of Morley's farm at Marsh Haddon. The barns were the home of the steam engines that the Morley's used for cultivation, also nearby was the van that travelled with the engines, and that was in quite good order.

Paradise Cottage had little to commend it in appearance, it was stone built, still very upright, but just a two-up, two-down farm cottage. Mrs Mabel Morley, widow of William Morley, kept the cottage for her once a year trip to Brize Norton. Inside she kept a few items of furniture, very little really for she never stayed more than a week or so. The water came from a pump in the front garden—there was neither drainage nor electricity, that came to the village in the 1930s. There were lots of fruit trees, both in the garden and in the delightful orchard behind, including a big walnut tree. It was a beautiful setting, but neglect caused its ruin, and the field was let to Upper Haddon Farm.

Gill Edwards outside her Paradise Cottage.

29

Fir Tree Cottage (pictured on the left) and (on the right) Marie Packer, Christabel Knight, Margaret Timms, Dicky Print, and Ray Knight.

On the west side of the little holding was a right of way leading to the 'Cuckoo Pen', so children were passing quite often, and without a doubt they helped themselves to some of the fruit. After all there was no one about, only birds—starlings and jackdaws by the hundreds. The footpath also led to the field named 'Cure All', so this would be the path that people would use if sickness came.

Later the furnished cottage was let at an exorbitant rent.

Outside the doors to *Paradise Cottage* and on the left-hand side, on the side of the road, was *The Cottage*—this was an extended part of Morleys, and the home of John Stone and his wife Leah, who had two young daughters, Sylvia and Christine. Mrs Stone had been in employment with the Morleys, and had been promised the cottage when it became empty—previously they had lived at Aston, where Mr Stone was employed in the Aston Laundry.

The Cottage was a grade two listed building, late sixteenth century, stone flags on the floors, ribbed doors, with thumb latches, winder stairs to left of passage—altogether a very old and interesting cottage, one of the oldest in the village—it had quite an attractive appearance out side but with just a small front garden.

John Stone lived to be eighty years old and died in 1972. Leah lived on well into her nineties which was surprising as she had always seemed a rather delicate lady. Notably, she kept her lovely dark hair which was a characteristic of her family.

Opposite Stone's cottage are two more very old cottages: *No. 1 and No. 2 Lilac Cottages*. At one time the date was on the outside, in front, in the form of a stone plaque, but a repair man unfortunately took a fancy to it and removed it—on it was carved, A.W. 1712. The cottages were part of the Astrop Farm on the Witney road, and it was one of the Christchurch, Oxford farms, they owned most of Brize Farms, except the Haddons, and the Glebe.

No. 1 Lilac Cottages was the home of Mr Rowland Timms, who lived there with his wife, daughter Janet, and sons Edwin and

The Cottage.

31

Sydney. Rowland, nicknamed Hummy, was an extraordinary man, he was very very clever with machinery, and he once made a motor plough with the help of Mr Print, the blacksmith. Farmers were interested in it, and he really should have had it patented. Rowland also made garden rotovators, just out of anything that was to hand and suitable—he even used motorbike wheels for them. He also charged up the accumulators that were used for the wireless at that time.

Rowland Timms (Hummy)
in his Oxon & Bucks Regiment uniform.

Rowland also liked to go off for a swim at Worsham. He would take others with him, including children, and that meant that they would have a bumpy ride in his home-made sidecar, because it was just made from a box. Kathy went with him once, bumping up the Green Lane or Ting Tang as it was called. Once there Rowland would strip-off and plunge in. He could swim well. Kathy just stood on the bank, before the exhilarating ride back to Brize. Sydney has added a bit to that; he said his father would sometimes bring home glow worms he had collected on the lane. His workshop was an Aladdin's cave, but he knew where everything

No 1 Lilac Cottage, where Rowland lived.

was. He was special, no doubt, and there will never be another Hummy.

No. 2 Lilac Cottages holds a very dim memory for Kathy, and Clare cannot remember it at all, although her sister Marie told her about it. It was the smallest shop in the village, and the only one where you could spend a farthing. It was all sweets. As it was only a small house to begin with the shop must have taken up most of the one living room.

Mrs Mary Ann Joynes (known as Polly), whose shop it was, was so short that she could only just see over the counter, however nothing could describe the feeling of anticipation as we pressed down the thumb latch on her door. The aroma of sweetness hung in the air, and Polly hovered waiting for us to make up our minds, what a choice, the sherbet dabs, or Sharps Creamie(sic) toffee for a halfpenny, or perhaps gob stoppers and aniseed balls, sweets too many to mention!

Polly died in 1925. Her husband, Edmund, followed her two months after—they said he died of a broken heart.

A family named Broughton moved in afterwards, they had

three or four sons, but Donald was the only one we knew well because he came to school with us.

After that it was Mr Charles James with his wife, daughter Bertha, and son Frederick (Sonny) who lived there. Mr James was an extremely good gardener, no doubt gaining his skill at Franchester Nurseries at Carterton where he worked.

Next on our trip through the village is a row of three cottages facing south. In the first lived James Abbott together with his wife. James was a rather odd, eccentric old man who was bad tempered, so he became a target for the young lads of the village to annoy. The tale goes that they once they put a lighted firework down his chimney; the boys of course were nowhere to be seen when he angrily opened his door—no doubt they were watching from a safe distance! James was up at the school next morning, and because no one would admit to the prank, the whole school suffered by having a long tedious lesson on behaviour.

James Abbott rode a bicycle with a box attached to the front, stating his age as as being eighty-one. He always wore a long row of medals on Armistice Day, held on the 11th of November, but he also wore them on Whit Monday when the church had a fête, after which he then followed behind the band as closely as possible. James died aged eighty-four, so his box was actually out of date by three years, but we must give him credit for gaining his medals in the First World War.

Next door to James Abbott lived the Woodley family, Arthur, his wife Gladys (a daughter of the Kinchen family over the road), their daughter Dora, and son Ronald. Arthur and Gladys went on to celebrate their golden wedding. Gladys died at the age of eighty-seven, while Arthur went on to the grand old age of ninety-six.

The third cottage right at the top of the row, was the home of Arthur Preston and his wife, but the only two children at home in our school years were his son John and daughter Iris. She unfortunately had the nickname Ikey. It was no secret that Arthur Preston liked his drink, and spent most night down at the 'Axe'. Mrs Preston made no secret of the fact either that she had to keep her purse tied around her neck because, as she was heard to say, "he would spend it all on drink!"

Just over the road was another row of cottages, level with the one where Jimmy Abbott lived. These were mostly occupied by the Kinchen family. In the first and the biggest of the cottages lived William Kinchen, his wife Rose and their daughter Gwen. The older children had all left home, and some lived not very far away.

Gwen had a nice singing voice that she'd had trained, she also played the piano, and was another who showed off her skills in the 'Axe'.

The next cottage in the row was where the Peacheys lived, Edie was a daughter of William Kinchen and his first wife. Edie's husband was Ernest, the children were called Denzil, Ralph, and Barbara and they all attended the village school.

Further up was yet another Kinchen daughter, who had married a Broadway and they had three daughters. Mr Broadway was a signalman at the station, but sadly he died very young and the family then moved away. Their house in the Kinchen row was very old and it had a stone winding staircase. The house always seemed to be a little detatched from the rest, and in time a division was made between it and the rest and it became a private property.

The next cottage up and backing on to the Kinchen's row was *Laburnam Cottage* and was another grade two listed building. Its occupants were Joseph and Tom Winfield, but after a while Joseph moved to live in Witney, while Tom married Daisy. Tom worked on the railway as a ganger, they were all Methodists and all had wonderful singing voices. The Laburnam is still in the front garden.

Sideways on to the road was another row of cottages which looked into the Winfield's garden.

In the first was Jack Kinchen, his wife, and their daughter Ada. Ada was the same age as Kathy and Clare. Their cottage was very small, only two up and one down. Jack started work as a very young lad, in Mr Packer's shop, (Clare's grandfather). He left Mr Packer at the age of sixteen to work for the Morleys, to drive a steam plough. He later worked for John Allen.

In the next cottage along was Ernest Faulkner and wife Nell, and their two sons Peter and Roger. Ernest became a sailor in the First World War. Nell was our Post-lady for a number of years, and then Ernest took over the postal duties and continued almost into his retirement years.

The top cottage changed tenants quite often, and it too was very small.

On the back of the previous cottages was a dairyman, Mr William Winfield; his house was quite large. He lived with his wife and three children, Perrin, Mary and Percy, who all went to school with Kathy and Clare. On the side of the house was the dairy, and Mr Winfield delivered milk to the village in a pony and trap—this was before the time of bottled milk, so people needed to put out their milk jugs onto the door steps. He used a large can with a one-pint measure and a half-pint one.

His fields were behind the Upper Haddon Farm fields, and one of them could have been the field named 'Cure All'. Later Mr Winfield moved to the Glebe Farm on the Burford Road.

This lower end of the village seemed to consist of rows of cottages, and we now come to one facing the road, and we are now looking over to Winfields. There were four cottages in the row, coming right out on to the path. In the first was our coal-man, Mr Joe Faulkner, who worked for Marriotts of Witney. The coal cost two shillings a bag, and was all there was at that time for heating the home. Women and children would go out into the fields with trucks and old prams in order to collect fallen twigs from under the hedges—this was mostly for kindling. It was Kathy's job as a small girl to get a bucket of small wood for her father to light the fire first thing in the morning. This had to be dry, and when that was lit small bits of coal could be added.

Mr Faulkner was a nice man, quiet and kind. His wife was kind too, for as well as having small boys of her own, she would have two or three children from the poor part of London for a few weeks in the summer. When they came we looked at their thin arms and legs, and oh they were so pale! However, by the time they went home, after spending time out in the fields and the sunshine, and with plenty of good food, they filled out and had a golden tan—they just did not look like the same children. Mrs Faulkner was so fond of children, and what a lovely way she had of showing it. Later they had more children of their own.

The next cottage in the row was where Min and Nelly Archer lived (which was mentioned earlier), they had the allotment at 'Gravel Pits'. Nelly was short and very very wide, and she liked to sit out on a chair on the pavement in the summer time, and watch the local people going by. Neither of them liked to miss anything that was going on around, so Min would start her conversation with "I happened to be at the window..." but they were good at heart, and would sit with the sick, and even mend clothes for mothers with big families. Clare and her sister always knew what was coming as they passed by. Min would quote a bit of scripture: "In the midst of life we are in death"—this was when they were nearly out of earshot.

The two top cottages in Min and Nelly's row, in our early days, was a carpenter and wheelwright's shop, belonging to a Mr Taylor. He did not live there, as his home was a few yards up the road. Looking into the shop we say as in most carpenters' shops, a mass of shavings, timber and sawdust, but the thing that remains in our memory of this place was the big black labrador dog. He would walk side by side with Mr Taylor when he went home, carrying a piece of timber in his mouth every day.

Later, the carpenter's shop was made into two cottages, the top and bottom of the row both being named as *Homelea No. 1* which at times led to rather heated arguments!

They all belonged to Miss Rosa Worley who we will be coming to next. Miss Worley's shop! It drew us like a magnet if we had a few pennies to spend. As we opened the door the hinged bell went 'ping!' it was all part of the magic. A totally different aroma greeted us, it was paraffin in a tank just behind the door, and for a while that was all we could smell, it pervaded throughout the shop.

Worley's Shop (above) circa 1950s and (below) Miss Rosa Worley.
Photo taken by Kathy from her front window (it's a daffodil in foreground in case you are wondering what it is!)

We looked down at the counter, which had a glass top, an array of shirt buttons, reels of cotton, knicker elastic, boot laces, safety pins, every small emergency was catered for. Notepaper and birthday cards, what a selection! Something to suit all tastes. Curled up on the top would be Puss, the cat.

Behind the counter were the Woodbines and Old Holborn tobacco, and the Red Bell plus cigarette papers.

The window held an assortment of china, all very pretty, and just right for a birthday

38

present. Behind us, up over the door, were the chamber pots—discreetly placed.

But that was not what we had come for; should we have some sweeties out of the big jars on the shelf, or perhaps there were sherbet dabs, aniseed balls, or a stick of licorice, whatever we decided, it was soon wrapped up and was probably in our mouths before we were out of the door.

Miss Worley was a real lady, and she expected us to behave ourselves and always to say, "please" and "thank you".

Apart from the shop, Miss Worley gave great support to the church and many other activities. She was secretary to the Women's Institute when it first started in the village and held the position for a some years.

For many years Miss Worley provided a kind of second home to her nephew Tom, and his sister Phyllis Worley, whose father had died so early in their lives. Phyllis particularly spent a great deal of her young life with aunt Rosa, mostly during the school holidays—her home was in Witney, but Brize was home too.

Living in the house with Miss Worley was Miss Silman, who sometimes helped in the shop, and Miss Harrex. All were related in some way, and all dressed in black, or so it always seemed to us as children.

Miss Harrex we believe came from Derbyshire, and so she spoke with a totally different accent. This hypnotised us at Sunday school where she gave firm teaching with Mrs Butler, and made sure that we all had a religious text to affix in a small album. Miss Harrex always walked through the village at a very brisk pace, wearing her large black hat and carrying a long black umbrella which she utilised as a walking stick—she appeared quite a person to be reckoned with.

Life to us as children seemed to be governed by church chapel or school.

To some lucky children invitations were given out to attend a party at the shop (it must have been Tom's or Phyllis's birthday). A nice tea was provided, which included some of Miss Worley's home cured ham. This had a special flavour and was absolutely delicious. Afterwards games like consequences and quiz games were played. Phyllis seemed to be in charge of the party and it would finish with a sing-song with all the guests joining in. Then we all went home happy and contented. Clare and Marie Packer joined in this fun and thoroughly enjoyed the kindness shown.

Over the road, facing Miss Worley's shop, was the black-smith's shop, a very busy place at times. Mr Albert Print was the blacksmith, and as one drew near you could hear the ringing of the hammer on the anvil. It had a rhythm all its own, a big tap followed by a smaller tap. Albert Print made the horse shoes himself, cutting the iron and heating it in his furnace, he then bent it over the anvil and got it to the right size for the horse that needed it. Mr Print was not a large man but he must have been very strong to manage the large horses that he shod.

Children liked to get in his smithy to have a warm in the winter time, and he would let them pump his bellows, some-times until the sparks flew. He also had a swing fitted in the shed-like room next to the smithy.

Farmers utilised Mr Print's skills to mend parts of their machinery, and he also sharpened and mended lawn mowers.

Behind the smithy, in a small shed, was another little hive of industry; Mr Castle from Ducklington soled and heeled boots and shoes, another necessity for the village.

Also behind the smithy was a cottage, nearly hidden from view. It was the home of Mr and Mrs Alfred Timms — they had a daughter, Pearl, and son, Gordon. Mr Timms

Albert Print, the Blacksmith.

40

was a skilled stonemason, and was also a very good and keen cricketer.

Behind the blacksmiths and Alf Timms' house were two more very old farm cottages, which belonged to Christchurch Oxford. In each of them lived a family by the name of Faulkner, but they were not related as far as we know.

In the further of the two lived Bert and Annie—both were quite short in stature and they were known as Little Tar and Mrs Tar. They had two sons, Norman (the eldest), and Frank (our whistling paper boy that we mentioned earlier). The family belonged to Brize Norton Methodist Chapel (Bert was a local preacher).

In the adjoining cottage lived Mr Fred Faulkner and his wife (pictured left) with their two daughters, Bertha, and Vera, who were both still living at home. Vera went with us to school, although she was a little older than we were.

Their home had a pump house attached on the end, which was always left open. Inside there was a pump, over the large sink, so those who had no well of their own

The two Faulkner Cottages, behind the Blacksmiths.

could go there with their buckets. It was at its busiest on a Monday morning—washing day. Fathers with families would start very early fetching their water, and going a good many times. As well as washing the clothes, the rinsing was done using a Reckett's blue bag to give the whites a brightness. The well never ever seemed to run dry.

In those days some wives were washer women for the larger families, a very hard life but the extra money was useful.

Also a good many wives did gloving. These were brought from Leafield and were already cut out but had to be stitched by hand. The reward was far too low, but it was something that could be done while sitting in front of the fire after the children were tucked up in bed.

Keeping to the same side as the smithy will bring you to a long driveway going up to *Yew Tree Cottage*, and the home of Mr Harry Smith and his wife. Mr Smith was a butcher, and halfway up that long drive was his building used for storing meat. We are not sure if it was a shop, or where he sold his meat.

Mrs Smith was a quiet lady, and was not seen about much in

the village. She did, however, find her way round the back way to Clare's orchard, and was allowed to help herself to the damsons that she liked so much.

About level with *Yew Tree* and across a drive, we come to an old cottage facing the old allotments. This was the home of three old bachelor brothers, Dicky, Teddy and Jimmy Kinchen. They must have been almost at retirement age when we knew them, not that we saw much of them. We do know that Dicky was the businessman and that he owned quite a few cottages. We do not think he liked to keep his money in banks, because if someone called asking him to settle a bill he would go upstairs and come down with a sackful of money! He made no secret of it, but admittedly he did occasionally walk to Witney sometimes, 'all of five miles', to visit a bank.

People who knew them better always told the same story (which sounds a bit outlandish these days); this was that they cooked their dinner in a pot on a hook suspended over the fire— into the pot would go meat and vegetables, plus the pudding, rolled-up in a cloth. It didn't do them any harm, because they all lived to a ripe old age.

Coming further on down the drive and on the right, was another old cottage, the home of the Ilotts. Unfortunately, we cannot remember them, nor their cottage which has since disappeared altogether.

Across the same driveway we find a very secluded cottage which was the home of Tom Bye and his second wife. His first wife died in 1926, she was just sixty-years old. The second Mrs Tom Bye did not mix with anyone much. When Tom died in 1943, it left his wife in the cottage alone and lonely, so then she was just pleased to see anyone should they call at her home.

Tom Bye was the father of Albert Bye who we wrote about earlier, and subsequently had his cottage named after him.

A cottage adjoining Tom Bye's house was one belonging to Pratt's Farm. A Mr Daniel Faulkner lived there. Clare and Kathy both remember his mother as a very, very old lady—Kathy was afraid of her, and didn't the old lady know it! When going home from school, Kathy would absolutely dread going past if the old lady was leaning over the gate, a favourite spot for her. She would have either a man's cap on, or an old fashioned bonnet tied under the chin—and knowing that Kathy was scared of her, in a kind of cackle she would utter: "I'll ave eee!" Kathy would then make for home as fast as her feet would carry her.

We go over the road to a special place. It really cannot be put into words what the field named 'Large Ground' meant to us as children, for not only the young, but people of all ages used it, and it was a playing field in the true sense. However, it was not as large as the name suggests. A well worn stepping stone, over a stone stile, beside a big farm gate [usually kept closed] led to the track where all the footpaths in the lower end of the village met. Just inside the stile was a large elm tree, this was a great thing on a hot day, and the little children, especially the girls, would gather here and play with their dolls. Others ventured further down the track to the stream, this was the same one that slowly flowed into Timms' orchard; here were plenty of little fish for those who had a net, while others might have a jam jar on a string—many a little minnow met it's end here!

There was a wide bridge over the stream where farmers could get their waggons across. This was where all the footpaths divided—you could go either left or right. Kathy can remember her grandfather, who was clerk of the council, saying: "Keep walking those footpaths or you will lose them." So there would be the young courting couples, strolling hand in hand to find a secluded place of their own and out of the range of eyesight, and families going for walks on Sunday evenings, aiming to get to Lew Barrow or at least to the railway line.

Every summer there were two camp meetings for the Methodist church, one in June and one in July. Notices were given out so that people who were interested would gather there ready. Mr Fred Field would have asked Mr Castle for permission to use the field known as 'Large Ground'.

Preparation was made for a big waggon to be in place under the big elm tree just inside the gate, and bales of hay were already up in the wagon for the Minister and speakers to sit on. There were also bales scattered around for people to sit on. The service would start with a well known hymn, then there would be readings from the Bible followed by a short address, a hymn for the children, and by this time there would be many people present as the Methodist church at that time was very strong.

It always seemed to be held on a lovely sunny day, and everyone looked happy to be there.

Kathy remembers going to just one of these meetings when she was taken by her aunt Norah, who held her hand and even took her up on to the waggon. Kathy had never experienced the enthusiasm of a camp meeting, it was much livelier than the services at Alvescot which she had been used to. She knew the children's hymns and joined in the singing and listened to the address and the prayers, and enjoyed being there, in fact, everyone seemed reluctant to be moving when it was over, and lingered a little longer under the old elm tree. After a while they all began to drift away and 'Large Ground' returned to normal. Now it is just a beautiful memory of village life as it once was.

'Large Ground' is gone now and in its place is a new estate called Chestnut Close. The footpaths were saved, however, and are now reached by going through the new estate.

Almost opposite 'Large Ground' is *Kithicks House*, built in 1691, at least that is the date on the chimney stack. It's the home of Mr and Mrs John Packer and their two daughters Marie and Clare.

The old house was a joy to live in, with a pleasant sitting room, and a farmhouse style kitchen, which was used for all meals and the preparation of food.

At one time there was an inglenook fireplace and a baker's oven. Mr Packer had this unit bricked up and a coal-fired cooking stove installed. There were only two bedrooms, but there were two attic rooms, used mostly for storage. To reach the bedrooms was a curved stone staircase, very chilly but impossible to carpet. Also included in the downstairs area was

Kithicks House.

what seemed to be a dairy, it was used as a 'walk-in' larder to store milk, butter, cheese and so on, and it always seemed very chilly in there too, but remember there were no fridges in those days, and everything stayed cool and fresh. That was home as the Packer family knew it. The old orchard was superb with Blenheim apples, greengages, plums and damsons, plus all the berried fruit, loganberries, and gooseberries.

Mr Packer was a skilled carpenter, wheelwright, and the village undertaker, as well as being a sidesman and a member of the church council at St Britius church, and also a bellringer. As a bellringer he rang at the appropriate time what was known as the death bell. This was rung about ten times to let the village people know that a poor soul had passed away.

Amongst other funeral accoutrements was a purple and gold 'Pall', a large drape which covered the coffin as it went into the

46

church on the bier. The bier was a very old but attractive way of getting the coffin to the church—it was the type with arched hoops on which flowers could be hung, not wreaths in those days. It sent the deceased through the village in a very simple an ornate way on their final journey.

To support the church and help with its costs a village fête was held in the *Vicarage* garden, and the big lawn was filled with stalls, plus bowling for the pig, and bowling for the teaset. Tea and cakes were also served in the old parish room by

The Packer family.

the ladies of the church, and not to be forgotten the lovely ice cream made by Mrs Sturch from Grange Farm.

Church life at Brize Norton was, to families and children, the social occasion where everyone met and talked over village happenings. The choir was very important, and the church had such a wonderful organist in Warren Green, who came from Bampton, and on special occasion would give an organ recital after evening service, when sometimes Clifford Bellinger would sing 'O for the Wings of a Dove' in his beautiful boy soprano voice.

Choir supper was one of the winter social gatherings when the choir and church members, and the vicar, gathered in the Victory Hut for a meal prepared by the ladies of the village, plus home made wine and beer! The highlight of the evening was when Mr Tom Pratt, the farmer, began to sing: 'The Mistletoe Bough'. Everyone waited, knowing that it would end up being sung very flat, but each and everyone clapped and knew, God willing, the same procedure would again take place next year.

The Victory Hut was an ex-army hut, erected at the end of the First World War as a general meeting place for village activities.

Choir outing was a village summer outing for the choir boys and their immediate families, the choir men and friends, church members and sometimes the vicar. They all went for the day out to Bournemouth, or maybe Weymouth, all with picnic baskets, and umbrellas in case it rained (which it rarely did), then came home again after calling in at a public house en-route to lubricate the voices of the choir, who sang all the way home!

Within the church, which is mainly of Norman origin, is a tomb of a crusader by the name of Sir John Daubigny. Children often looked at him, not really understanding why he was there, also taking the liberty of 'sitting' on the edge of his tomb, to wait for the signal to blow up the bellows of the organ.

The children's Sunday School was mostly held in the Parish room because it had been erected in part of the *Vicarage* garden, otherwise it was held inside the *Vicarage* in a small sitting room, with the fire going. Children liked it in the summer time when the Sunday School was held in the garden under the big chestnut trees, and went home with bunches of flowers that Mrs Butler (the vicar's wife) had allowed them to gather. What a lovely way to teach children Christianity and the Bible stories.

As a wheelwright, a skilled and precise job, Mr Packer repaired all the farm carts and the yellow coloured Cotswold waggons; it was hard work. Mr Print the blacksmith always helped to get the metal rims fixed, and children watched in awe at the size of the fire that was needed to get the metal rims to expand before they could be dropped on to the wheels, which had been placed on a special metal circle in the big yard.

As children, Marie and Clare were always searching for something different and one day they found a Boer War soldier's helmet, tucked in a recess in the old workshop. Unfortunately, it was too old and delicate to be repaired, and was disposed of.

Next to *Kithicks*, Clare's home, was a very small cottage,

almost hidden away. This was the home of Mr Taylor the carpenter and wheelwright, who had the black Labrador dog we wrote of earlier. Mr and Mrs Taylor were quite old, but then thinking back, anyone over thirty seemed old to us! However, this is where the black dog would bring his mouthful of wood.

Next door to them were the Cambray family, Frank and his wife and sons, Edward and John, and daughters, Mary and Joan. Frank was a signalman at Bampton Station. Kathy can just about recall Frank's father living in the cottage with them.

Over the road were two families, the nearest to the road were the Archer family. Mrs Archer was a widow, her husband was sadly killed on the last day of the First World War. She lived with her two daughters, Mary and Rose, and her son Ernest. Clare tells the story about when the family hired a gramophone from Mr Kempster of Witney and they played the tunes of the twenties, so Clare being just over the road would get as close as she could without being seen, and listened too!

Next door was the Field family, Caleb and Polly. Their music was of an entirely different kind, as they were members of the Methodist church, and had the most beautiful singing voices, especially Caleb. All the Field family were excellent singers, so no doubt they were more used to Charles Wesley hymns than the ones that came from next door.

The Archer's (known as the 'gramophone players') home, nearest to the road. Adjoining them was the Field family home.

Around the corner from the gramophone players were a group of cottages. Leading in from the entrance from the road, right at the back were the Clarke family, Mr and Mrs Clarke, with daughters Phyllis, Frances and Doreen, and sons Roy, Ronald and Laurence. They were a quiet family. All the children went to school with Clare and Kathy.

Another little cottage was tucked away out of sight and this was where Chistabel Knight was born. The house on the roadside was the home of the Parkers, but where they came from we were not sure as Mrs Parker's dialect was strange to us and she talked very quickly. She had three daughters, Wyn, Mabel and Eve—another daughter, Ethel, had married Mr Frank Cambray who lived over the road. There were also two sons, Jimmy and Bert.

A little story about Wyn, she would strip off and wash upstairs in front of the window, and the allotments were just over the road so it could not be missed! They did say she had a very good figure.

There was yet another cottage tucked away on the roadside, and here lived Mr Harry Timms. He had a long white beard, and was the pig killer. When he came to Kathy's home she and her sister were ushered upstairs, the curtains were drawn and they were told not to look, but when the squealing started they just had to have a peep, and horror stricken they saw the knife and the blood! Both heads quickly went under the pillows—after all, they had been told not to look, and that it was no good to make a fuss. Then they were given this horrid bladder to play with, but the boys from *Diddely Corner* were not so fussy, they took scraps of pig meat home for their parents and even the chitterlings. Kathy's mother made lovely faggots with herbs, and home made lard with rosemary to season it. Kathy's father salted bacon and some was sold in the shop.

After the pig killer Timm's house, following up the road were four cottages called *Bognor Terrace*. In the second one lived Mr and Mrs Harry Miles. They were both elderly and when they died they left a sum of money to the church for a clock to be put on the church tower. However, on inspection the tower was found not suitable for a clock, so the money was put in trust for the children of the village leaving school.

The next tenant was Mr Print the blacksmith who lived there with his wife, and their son Richard. Later they moved to take over the Post Office, and Mrs Print became post mistress. In the next cottage lived Mrs Caroline Upstone, who became quite a character in her later years. It is believed that she was a First World War widow, and left to bring up her family on her own— we are not sure just how many children she had, but James her son married a Delnevo girl from Witney. Caroline became quite eccentric, and was noted for her wrinkled stockings and a compulsion for picking up cigarette ends. It was quite sad really but she was very old and had reached ninety-two when she died.

There was also a small cottage tucked away around the corner—a poor one, and nobody stayed there for long.

We now come to Barnes' bottom shop, it was one of two that the Barnes family had, and to the family that Kathy belonged. She lived at the bottom shop until she was three, with her father Mr Albert Barnes, her mother Lydia and her sister Muriel, her grandmother and her aunt Norah who also helped in the shop. Here they sold bread made in the *Bakehouse* (up by the church) by her grandfather, and also groceries, fruit and sweets.

Barnes 'Bottom Shop'

Kathy and her family lived in *Chichester House*, quite old with low ceilings, lots of outbuildings and a lovely orchard. Their water came from a pump outside the backdoor.

When Kathy was three-years-old her family moved down to *Colebrook Villa*, below the Station.

Colebrook Villa, named by the previous occupant, was very different to *Chichester House*, there was piped water pumped daily from the pump house just down the road, it was a comparatively new house that the station master had been living in, but he had moved to Bampton.

Kathy well remembers the day they moved although she was only three-years-old at the time. It was September, and she was put on the front lawn and told not to move. She sat and watched the butterflies on the Michaelmas daisies.

This house had hot water on tap upstairs and down, a bathroom, water lavatories, and lots of space. There was a garden front and back and also a big orchard. However, it was very lonely. Kathy had a sister two years older than herself, and also a little brother not yet one when they moved, it was very sad because he had been brain damaged when born, and he never walked or talked so he took up a lot of their mother's time, and he could not be left, especially as he got older.

Barnes' Shop from the Church Tower, showing only petrol pump in village.

They were a musical family and entertained on Sunday evenings, when friends came and they all sat round the piano. Kathy and Muriel, her sister, both had piano lessons from Miss Taunt from Bampton, and they also had violin lessons until Kathy slid along the dining room floor one day and broke all the pegs off. She recalls being very frightened, and wondering what her father was going to say when he returned home. Her mother broke the news and told him that it was all a complete accident, because she had polished the floors too much!

Kathy was only five when she started the long walk to school each weekday. Because there were no school dinners her grandparents would give Kathy and her sister a nice hot dinner each day, which was cooked in the *Bakehouse* oven. Grandpa would come wearing his big white apron carrying a tray with the lovely food, and they had to eat it all up—even greens and fat meat! Kathy loved her schooldays and so did Clare.

Across the road from Barnes' lower shop, (their main shop being further up the village) is *South Terrace*, believed to be owned by the Mark Timms who, with his wife and daughter Margaret, enjoyed living in the largest cottage at the far end of the row. The terrace had been built by a Mr Eggleton, known to Margaret as uncle Eggleton. Kathy and Clare are not sure which side of the family this man came from. In earlier times the terrace had been known as *Eggleton's Row*. Margaret's mother

South Terrace (faced Barnes' Bottom Shop).

53

sadly died, and in time she married Mr Ted Savory. Mr Timms
had been the lead cornet player in the days of the village band,
and at times and most Sundays would regularly play the cornet
loudly and well, but it thoroughly destroyed any thought of
Sunday afternoon rest for the neighbours.

The next cottage was let to a family named Archer, who
consisted of a widow with her small children, and who came to
the village from Langley, (a collection of cottages close to
Leafield)—they arrived at the time of the lease of Manor Farm,
changing from the Castle family to the Wilkins family.

The Phipps family lived in the next cottage. Clare can only
remember an elderly person with one son Jacky. Then a daughter, a qualified nurse, came home to nurse either mother or
father, Clare is not sure which. Nurse Phipps stayed until Jacky
married Mrs Archer from next door—at times Jacky would go
out on the allotment plot in front of the cottages to dig the
vegetable garden, he would then get tired, sit in his wheelbarrow and go to sleep, much to the glee of the other gardeners
and especially the children.

Next came Jim Mills, known as 'Tanky', and his wife. Jim was

Oxfordshire Steam roller and its road members in the village.

a great character who thoroughly enjoyed his allotment plot at the back of the cottages. He was a wonderful gardener and at the top of the plot was a large pig sty, of interest to the other allotment holders who all wanted manure for their gardens.

Alongside the pig sties was a large bench, where all and sundry would sit and talk over the condition of the pigs, the growth of plants, and the weather. And all helped along by a few bottles of beer and a lot of laughter. Country life at it's best!

When the time came for a pig to be slaughtered, it would be killed, scorched over a large fire, cut into joints, and Mr Mills would then very generously give all his neighbours either a small joint of pork, or chops, sometimes liver, and was greatly enjoyed by all.

The last cottage was alongside the road and was occupied by another Mark Timms and family; he was known as Darkie Mark because of his black hair, and also to distinguish him from the other Mark Timms. His son, Eric, lived with them, but the other members of the family had married and moved away.

Behind *Colebrook Villa* was a field that was used as an allotment; medium sized, with a wide strip of grass through the middle, and each side divided into strips. It was much used when Kathy was a young girl.

The land had the name of 'Platt', although originally it was known as 'Poors Plot'. In the distant past it was given to the widows of the village of Brize Norton—it came from a charity connected to the church of St Britius, but we were unable to find out who donated it in the first place. It must be recorded in the church records somewhere. It was very good growing land, the soil being different to the soil of that in the village, and it bordered on Norton Ditch, the village boundary.

Just a high hedge divided it from Kathy's orchard and back garden, so they were not overlooked. They could hear the chatter and smell the bonfires. It grew wonderful vegetables, and Mrs Parker was often seen pushing her wheelbarrow, overflowing with large carrots and potatoes and flowers, up the Station Hill on the mile to her home in the village. Clare says Mrs

Parker gave a lot away and often came round to her home with vegetables given freely.

Many of the cottages such as Mrs Parker's (she was a widow), had no garden at all, so her plot on 'Platt' was most important to her. Of course, Mrs Parker was not the only one that used it but names have been forgotten. There were, however, many bonfires and patches of colour where the flowers were grown.

In time they dropped off, one by one, Mrs Parker being the last to give up her plot. The land then was rented by Lower Haddon Farm, the money being used for winter coal given to widows, so another custom died out.

There were a good many plots on the allotments at the back of *South Terrace*: it was good growing land. It was bordered by the road on one side and the land ditch on the other, so that there was always water available. It came from the same stream going on to the 'Cuckoo Pen', also an attraction for the children, who would help themselves to a bit of rhubarb sometimes!

Right next to it were the *Elderbank Cottages*, just two of them. In one were two Bellenger brothers, and in the other an old couple by the name of Seacole. These cottages were in the field named 'Benny', which was usually cultivated. That field became very important a good many years later when it was turned into the village playing field, and the lovely Elderbank Hall was built to replace the old Victory Hut.

Before this the playing field was in 'Gassons' (a field opposite the Manor), but only when not in use by the farmer, and not in any state for cricket or football to be played.

We cannot say much about the *Chequers* public house, other than it seemed to be popular with some people, having a totally different atmosphere to that of the 'Axe'. The young footballers favoured the 'Axe' more, as did the cricketers; not so much larking about went on at the *Chequers*. Sometimes when the Berkshire Hunt met in the village—usually on the church green—they would move off to the *Chequers* where drinks would be handed round on a tray by the barmaid, Miss Alice Cuss; she was kept very busy.

Phone: Carterton 224.		BRIZE NORTON, OXFORD.

31 – 12 - 1947

Mr Arthur Timms. Leys Cottage

DR. TO

A. E. PRINT,
General Smith and Welder.

1947

			£	s	d.
July	14	2 ¾" to Draw-bar.	2	0	
	23	Drilling plate & 4 Gutter Bolts	1	0	
-	24	New handle to Shovel	3	6	
-	26	Fitting new Key & Collar to tractor plough	8	6	
	28	1 only 1" Stop valve	3	6	
Oct	16	New to Bed York.	4	0	
	23	New handle & Grinding slasher	4	6	
Nov	12	Steel tipping 2 Plough Shares	8	0	
-	21	" " 1	4	0	
		Paid Jan 17th 1948	1	19	=

A bill for work done by the Blacksmith, Mr Print, in 1947.

The schoolchildren were let outside to view this occasion. They took in all the details, particularly what the ladies were wearing... such strange garb, with their hair tied back in a strange bun, over which was worn a little black hat with a veil. They would be dressed all in black, but the men wore pink, not scarlet, and of course the hounds were eager to get going!

The ladies always rode side-saddle.

It would be a field day for the village ladies like Mrs Luckett who was always out first, armed with her bucket and a spade. She was followed by Mrs Harris. All good stuff for the garden!

On our travels up through the village it was quite likely we would see Benny Clements—he came from Witney, we believe. He had a flat cart with no cover, and his main sale would be paraffin. On his cart there would be other things, perhaps not all of it new, things like rat traps and a few garden tools, nothing of any quality. He was, however, sometimes asked for a special item. One day someone had asked him for a chamber pot! Yes, he could get one he said, and what better place to obtain one than at Miss Worley's shop. Once in there and confronted by the lady assistant he became flummoxed, and unsure what to ask for. In the end he asked for a piano! Miss Worley eventually cottoned on to what it was he wanted and produced a chamber pot—was it an association of words? a P, and a po? Anyway, ever after they knew just what he wanted when he asked for a piano!

There was also the scissor grinder, who came around about once a year, with a gadget on his bike that enabled him to sharpen. He asked only for a shilling or two, but it was not a good job as one had hoped for, the items he sharpened never seemed much good afterwards.

* * *

School Folk dancers showing banners (circa 1930s) – see next chapter.

Chapter 4

The School

Brize Norton is very lucky to have such a well built and pleasant school. It was opened in 1876 by the forefathers of the Timms' family. It was, and still is, the centre of the village activity.

Kathy and Clare arrived at the school on the same day, welcomed in by Miss Scrivens, who was in charge of the infants class. She was a very kind lady, who taught the children the alphabet and simple arithmetic.

We were given trays of sand in which we outlined the letters and figures, after which we graduated to a slate and slate pencil, and so by the time we were about six we all had the basic skills of reading, writing and arithmetic.

Moving up to standard one and two, we were then taught by Mrs Jones, the wife of the Headmaster, who was a most clever and patient teacher of Welsh descent. She taught the class very carefully to appreciate poetry and art, and to write and spell correctly. The poems had to be learnt by memory, so if asked, a child could stand up and recite to the class without hesitation. It gave the child confidence .

The vicar came occasionally to make sure that the children were knowledgeable about the Ten Commandments and so on.

Standard three and four were taught by Miss Hopkins, who taught us very carefully, the precise manner in which to write and compose a letter. The paragraphs were explained, verbs and adjectives explained, dots, commas, exclamation marks, all taught, never to be forgotten. With Miss Hopkins, further knowledge of arithmetic was taught, and both geography and history.

At about nine years old, scholars moved up to the Headmaster's class. Mr L. S. R. Jones had a very strong and powerful personality, and soon acquired the name of 'Boss' Jones, which

Mr Jones with the pipe band (circa 1930s).

stayed with him all his days at Brize Norton. Children were expected to absorb his quick and rather abrupt manner of teaching, but it was good.

As a Welshman he taught music and drama to quite a high standard; the garden scene from a Midsummer Nights Dream was performed on the school lawn as a fund raising event for the school. The costumes were all true theatrical style dress. They were loaned (or hired) from either the Oxford Drama Company, or the Oxford Theatre. Mr Jones was determined that things were all presented in as perfect a style as possible, so the asse's head was just perfect for Bottom the Weaver!

Music was the Headmaster's true love and the school choir won almost every competition they entered. Banners draped the school walls, certificates were fixed to any spare wall space.

Some of the success was achieved because a child chosen for the school choir was expected to be able to sing alone, it ensured Mr Jones could be sure of a true note, and no sharps or flats.

True to his Welsh origin, 'The Land of our Fathers' was taught in Welsh, which mystified everyone, then came the 'French National Anthem' and another French country song—this was a very varied choice of music for country children. Of course, English songs were taught as well. 'Nymphs and Shepherds'

Sewing class in Brize Norton school. Clare (far right) and Kathy (3rd from right).

being one of the regular tunes sung. Next on his list came the School Band: recorders were made by the boys out of various sizes of bamboo tubes. The recorders were set at perfect pitch by Miss Hopkins banging away on middle C on the school piano, and the finger holes adjusted until perfect. A violin was made in the carpentry department. At Christmas concerts at the school the music was mostly provided by the band, and carols and well known tunes were sung with great success.

Then came dancing. How the children loved dancing around the maypole, weaving very clever patterns with the ribbons. Morris dancing and Scandinavian style dancing was taught, and also English country dancing: 'Rufty Tufty' and 'Gathering Peascods' are two that come to mind.

While teaching Morris dancing, Mr

School production of Midsummer Night's Dream.

Jones learned of the skills of one Jinky Wells and his fiddle. He came from Bampton and he knew many of the old Morris tunes by heart, and so Jinky Wells was invited up to the school. Kathy and Clare were there. At the same time Mr Jones had asked Mr Cecil Sharp from Oxford to come to listen and translate most of the tunes being played—up until then, no written record had been kept.

Never to be forgotten was the patience shown to the children in teaching them mathematics to a degree not known before. Many children progressed on to either Burford or Witney Grammar School. Children who were not so academic were given the chance to show their skills, either at gardening (for the boys), or sewing and art design (for the girls).

As a last thought, hygiene was given a special emphasis. Each morning after prayers, Mr Jones' inspection of hand and finger nails was a regular occurrence—and sometimes teeth were looked at. Then, horror of horrors, the school dentist who would arrive once a year! Two treadle-operated drills were set up in what was usually the infant's class, and for the price of one shilling, children's teeth were examined and the necessary treatment given. A dreadful ordeal, but a most important form of care. One dentist acquired the worrying name of 'killer Cook'!

Coming out of school in the early Spring, children would gather together and play a game, 'Sheep, sheep, come home'. Two lines were drawn across the road with a piece of soft limestone (no chalk available at Brize Norton then). A gap of about fifty yards divided the lines. One child stood behind one chalk line, and he or she was the 'shepherd'; one child was 'the wolf' and would hide in a garden, while the rest of the children were 'the flock' of sheep, lined up behind the other chalk line.

The Shepherd would call: "Sheep, sheep, come home."
The flock of sheep replied: "We can't, we are afraid."
The shepherd then asked: "What of?"
The flock replied: "The wolf."
The shepherd calls: "The wolf has gone to Devonshire, and will not be back for seven years, so sheep, sheep, come home."

Gardening for the boys in 1928.

The response was a quick dash of the 'flock of sheep' to get to the shepherd before the wolf could catch one. If caught, that child became the wolf, and the whole procedure would start again. Maybe this game was a pattern picked up from the shepherds and their sheep in the surrounding meadows—who knows?

One must realise in these early days that there were no cars on the roads to injure the children, neither did there seem to be any bullying amongst the children.

Scandinavian dancers.

To add to the fun, Clare had a pair of very tall stilts made for her by her father in his workshop. The stilts caused great fun, and Clare coped by having a quiet garden to practise in. After a while the stilts got loaned out to other children, but most of them fell off, to the great glee of the other children watching.

No one seemed to have time to be bored, in fact no one ever used the word, because in amongst other fun, the seasons moved on to haymaking, whereby we all followed the cutter round, then it was harvest (there was no combine harvesters in those days), so we all trouped around after the cutter, which cut the corn and tied it up in bundles. We then helped to stand the sheaves up in stooks, and later came the noise of the threshing machine, and once again we all joined in.

* * *

Threshing at Manor Farm.

Chapter 5

Around the Church

The Church of Saint Britius is situated more or less in the centre of the village. It is a very solid looking building, with a square tower which has no battlements—this is quite unusual in a tower of this period. The peal of six bells called worshippers to church, each Sunday at eleven o'clock, and again at six o'clock. If there was an early communion service the Ting Tang bell was used.

The church is divided and has some thirteenth century portions but it is mainly Norman with a nice Norman porch entrance, Inside it is dominated by very large stone pillars, but has a very decorative altar, and two very pleasant stained glass windows. The rood screen separating the nave from the chancel is considered one of the best in the district.

St. Britius Parish Church.

We have mentioned before the tomb of Sir John Daubigny which is placed at the rear of the organ—a very nice organ too and it was well used at all services.

Sometimes at morning service a great upheaval occurred with the arrival of Miss Knight who was wheeled in wrapped in rugs, in a large bath chair, the size of which had to be seen to be believed. She was wheeled in by Miss Charlock, her housekeeper, and had been pushed uphill and downhill from the far northern end of the village—it certainly gave the children something to stare at in amazement.

The service was conducted by the vicar, Mr Butler, who with his wife lived at the *Vicarage*, a large house close to the church, along the Carterton road. Mr Butler would preach wonderful sermons, and was also a writer of some theological books, considered by some to be very important documents. Mr Butler was addressed officially as Reverend Butler.

Miss Mills was quite an important member of the community, and she lived in a pleasant cottage called *Watchman's Cottage* by the pathway called the 'Pop Socket', which was next to the cemetery and very central to the village. Miss Mills was a seamstress and dressmaker, and would do any alterations to

The Vicarage.

coats or dresses. Both Clare and Kathy had clothes made and altered by Miss Mills. Clare remembers having a posh white dress made for her confirmation service at the church.

It was a very interesting house to visit, always having a smell of new material and beeswax, which we believe was used to stiffen the fabrics. A large sewing machine took pride of place in the sewing room, plus the large paraffin lamp that gave off its own odour. As for the age of Miss Mills, it was difficult to decide—she seemed very, very old to us children, wearing long black clothes, with her hair pulled back in a bun shape with endless hairpins I think we were always rather in awe of her, with her talking with a mouthful of pins. We were never sorry to be going out of the door and would wait to see what concoction would come out of the visit.

Opposite the *Vicarage* is a pleasant house called *Homestead*. In our youth it was occupied by two mature sisters: the Misses, King. Both regular churchgoers, and involved in starting the Women's Institute, very popular with the women of the village.

Church Cottage.

Inscription on the tombstone of the blacksmith, John Silman, in the old churchyard.

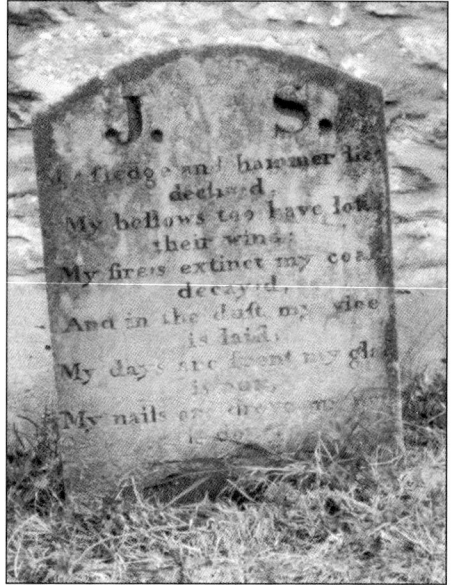

J.   S.

My sledge and hammer lies
declin'd
My bellows too have lost
their wind:
My fire's extinct my coals
decay'd
And in my dust my vice
is laid:
My days are spent my glass
is run,
My nails are drove my work
is done.

* * *

Chapter 6

Brize Farms & Barnes' Shops

Most of the farms in Brize Norton are owned by Christchurch College, Oxford, the largest being the Manor Farm. A high wall ran along the roadside which had big elm trees that were kept lopped, and these were known locally as the twelve apostles (although we think there may have been thirteen!).

Mr Castle was the farmer. He and his wife had two sons and a daughter—sadly both boys were killed in the First World War, leaving the one daughter, Miss Mary Castle.

Mr Castle owned a very big black horse, on which he used to ride around the fields to inspect the crops and stock. Children of the village would wait eagerly by the gate opening on to the roadway, then hopefully if they opened the gate, 'Daddy Castle' as he was known, would toss coins for them to collect. Unfortunately, neither Kathy nor Clare were allowed to join in this fun.

Farmer Mr Castle on his horse, Elderbank Cottage, and 'Benny's Field'
(all fields locally had names but no one had any idea as to who 'Benny' was).

The Manor House in 1915.

The day of the sale of the household goods when Mr Castle died was fascinating. Most of the goods were displayed on the large front lawn, and Clare can remember playing a simple tune on a old spinet, a very squeaky small piano.

Grange Farm was occupied by the Sturch family, John his wife and two daughters, Ruth and Mary, (Mary was at school with

The Twelve Apostles (the tall Elm trees outside the Manor House gardens).

70

Clare and Kathy). Ruth was older and had gone to Burford School. Mr Sturch was a church warden, a strong supporter of the church and attended most Sundays.

Grove Farm is situated on the outskirts of the village, almost in Minster Lovell. It was occupied by Mr William Badger, his wife and four children, Michael, Joan, Alec and Phyllis. Only Alec and Phyllis were at school with Kathy and Clare. Again very strong supporters of the church. Mr Badger was the second church warden, and always attended Sunday morning church.

The Glebe Farm was so far out of the village that we saw very little of the Fowler family. Mrs Fowler had been a Jenny Timms, she died very young—and by 1935 Mr William Winfield had moved in with his young family, Perrin and Percy, and Mary. This farm is owned by the church, but Mr Winfield and family were Methodists.

Astrop Farm, alongside the Witney road, was occupied by the Kenlock family. Mr Kenlock, his wife and one son Peter, again a Christchurch-owned farm.

Kathy's great grandfather, Arthur Barnes, bought the shop by the church in 1873, and it stayed in the Barnes family for nearly one hundred years. Arthur Barnes died in 1919, the year before Kathy was born, and the shop was left to his two sons: John, the eldest, managed the grocery side, and William, Kathy's grandfather, the bakery side. Although they worked along together, the bakery was on the opposite side of the road to the grocery. This hardly mattered until the time when motorcars first appeared, then you had to take great care as it was a junction, with roads leading off to Bampton, Carterton and Burford. (Wally Barnett had just started his weekly bus to Witney market, when he was unfortunately involved in an accident – see p.77).

On entering the shop you were always greeted with, "Can I help you?" It was not a shop where you could wander in and help yourself—most people brought a list, which they would hand over to whoever was serving, that had a proper ticket made out with a proper heading; 'A. Barnes & Sons' . It was all added up, paid, and receipted.

Barnes' shop billhead in 1955.

They did get asked for some strange things at the shop: one man requested "black man's socks, and white men's handkerchiefs"! Violet Upstone always and only wanted Nestlés chocolate...

One day the two Miss Mills came in—Ada and Nelly. Ada always stood right behind Nelly, and would utter things that she herself wanted. On one occasion it was some paste to make sandwiches:

"But er don't like fish", said Nelly.

"What else 'ave you got?"

"Yes, that will do. Sardine and tomato... 'cos er don't like fish."!

Some old men would come in to buy snuff, a pinch put in a three cornered bag for a few pence. Then there was Mrs Luckett! She listed the things that she needed:

"Brooke Bond Divinity tea"!

They began to get the other things ready first and then would ask her once again, "What kind of tea was it, Mrs Luckett?"

"That there Divinity tea", she replied.

She meant 'Dividend', of course!

Other strange things that were asked for were:
dromedary sugar, 'gestive biscuits and another kind of tea—this time it was 'Typhoid'!

They also sold meat, and on a Saturday they would be open until ten o'clock at night. There would be a last minute rush, just in case Mr Barnes might be selling off any meat cheap, because it might not last until Monday.

Right up until 1930 they had salt delivered in blocks by a

woman driving two horses and a big flat cart, and shouting like mad. She stood up most of the time, cracking her whip. Children were frightened stiff of her—she was the 'Salt Woman'!

Early on, biscuits were sold loose—none were in packets— and came in decorative tins which were displayed in the window to make a window dressing. Piled three tins high, some people only wanted half-a-pound, and it was sure to be from one of the bottom tins! Sultanas were also sold loose, from wooden boxes, and bananas came on the stem and were called 'hands'.

To cap it all the place was infested by mice and a number of traps were set every night, but it was impossible to keep them out. The barley, which was kept for the pigs, was blamed for the numbers of mice, even though it was stored outside up in the granary.

There was a drapery department, where skeins of wool would be sold for sixpence. Also, Holdfast boots, which were very hard wearing for the working man, these cost twelve shillings and sixpence. Usually a woman would be serving in the drapery department, but if no one was there someone would open the dividing door into her house and shout "DRAPERY PLEASE!"

Everything was wrapped up in brown paper—this hung on the end of the counter in a long roll, and it was tied up with string, Kathy helped in keeping the string free from knots.

One funny story that must not be missed, is when Kathy's father had to fill the little pepper drawer. This had a small brass scoop to convey it into the tiny bags. Luckily he was in the office doing this—always a sneezy job!— when he dropped the full drawer! The pepper rose up and Kathy's father began sneezing, and making such a noise that Betty Giles in the shop went to see what was going on. She too quickly began to sneeze, and they both made a hasty exit. With tears streaming down their faces, they both went into fits of laughing and became quite hysterical!

On the ceiling of the shop were lots of hooks with all sorts hanging from them: saucepans, brushes, oil-cans and grass cutters—you name it and there it was. Kathy's cousin, Gordon was a dab hand with the long pole needed to retrieve these articles, and people would hold their breath as he reached for something difficult, but he always managed to get it down safely, sometimes catching it with his free hand; it was years of practice that had given him this skill.

Going into the house from the drapery department, you went into a spacious hall, with an old fashioned big front door that went into the large garden. The house with its big rooms was always a busy place, as all business premises are. The long staircase went up to many bedrooms, and this reminds Kathy of the lovely Christmas parties they had there, because upstairs were things in big cupboards such as drapery items that had not sold over the years, and they were allowed to use these for dressing up and playing charades (one of Kathy's favourite games). They played in great big hats all out of fashion, long gowns and shoes for big feet—they were so good those parties.

Over the road from the shop was the bakery. Kathy was more familiar here with her grandfather, her uncle George and, of course, her father.

Mr W. A. Barnes, Kathy's grandpa.

Kathy's grandfather was a cheerful man, always singing —usually the old Irish lullaby, 'Tu-ra-lu-ra-lu-rah' (that was what it sounded like anyway!), as he busied himself in the bakehouse. Uncle George made the dough for bread, dough cakes and lardy cakes, for which Barnes's were well-known. Mr Fred Giles made buns and doughnuts, and the hot cross buns. These he would start making at 4 a.m. and they sold at seven for six-pence.

The buns were delivered

74

through the village by Kathy's father, then going on to Bampton and Black Bourton, Alvescot and Carterton, then they would go up to Minster Lovell.

The bread round (which Kathy used to go on with her father) sometimes took the same route on Tuesday's and Thursday's. Kathy would help out by going to some of the houses—she never forgot the telling-off her father gave her once, when she let a farmer's wife change a Tuesday's loaf for a fresh one on a Thursday!

Albert and Lydia Barnes, Kathy's parents.

Christmas cakes were made using their recipe, and Kathy's uncle George would decorate them with icing—a lovely sight when they were all laid out on a bench.

Kathy and Muriel with dad at Colebrook Villa.

In the early days the deliveries were made by horse-drawn vans, usually two horses were used. On coming home the horses would be fed and watered and brushed down by Cecil Broughton, who would also have cleaned out the stable.

The Barnes family were all strict Baptists, and attended the strict Baptist Chapel at Alvescot, however, gradually the younger ones left and went to either the Methodist or to the Parish church at Brize Norton.

The Poplars was where Kathy's grandfather lived. There were two unmarried sons there and one daughter. The house, built by Joseph Timms in 1900, was for John Barnes (the older son of Arthur), when he was to be married. Arthur Barnes died in 1919, and his son then moved into the shop, while Kathy's grandfather moved into The *Poplars*.

The Poplars (Barnes shop at bottom) c.1920.

It was not far from the *Bakehouse*—where Kathy had her dinners on schooldays—it was a big house, very close to the back of the church. Kathy sometimes stayed the night with her sister Muriel. If it was a bell ringing practise night, it was dreadful, no peals to be heard only a cacophony of jangled noise—no sleep until they had finished!

They had some wonderful Christmas parties when all the family were at home, everything was arranged for the children, and there were a good many of them! All the aunts and uncles and their children would come. They usually started with a brantub in the afternoon, going on to party games, and carol singing. Grandpa Barnes was so happy to see them all there having a good time, although he had lost his wife in 1923, (she was the one that had helped in the bottom shop). Kathy looked forward to that Christmas party from one year until the next. After a party finished they were so tired, Kathy and Muriel, that they could never remember getting back home to Colebrook.

Close to the church, going off from the Carterton road, was Moat Farm. It was where the Field family lived—Mr and Mrs Field and their five daughters; Mary (Polly), Elizabeth, Olive, Lucy and Eva. It was not a real farm as such, but there was an old attractive Cotswold barn and big farmyard.

Sadly they lost their daughter Olive in 1926 in a freak road accident. Mr Wally Barnett from Carterton had just started the very first bus to run from Carterton to Witney market on a Thursday, and as he was coming round the *Bakehouse* corner, Olive was coming in the opposite direction—her attention was taken by poplar tree being lopped close to the church, when the accident happened. Sadly, Olive died. Her little sister, Lucy, who had been with her, saw everything. An enquiry was held in the Field's kitchen and Mr Barnett was totally exonerated.

Wally Barnett's bus with girls going to cookery class at Bampton.

Mr Fred Field was carter for Mr Castle at the Manor; he looked after twelve horses. He would go out in the morning at 5 a.m. to feed them, then come home and have his breakfast and then go back to work at 6 a.m. Mr Castle had two other horses (these were his riding horses for going round the farm), and were looked after by Mr Eden who lived in the little cottage between The *Bakehouse* and The *Poplars,* where Kathy's grandfather lived.

The threshing was done in the farmyard at Moat Farm. All the ricks of straw were there. Jack Hunt carried the straw to make the ricks, while the chaff went to the stables, and the sacks of corn were taken to the barn and emptied into large heaps. At harvest time, horses and wagons were in and out of the yard all day long. When the empty wagons went back to the fields, Eva and Lucy took milkcans of tea to their father at fields named 'Nine Acre', 'Sandpit', 'Weavers Ground' and others, then they would walk back home. Extra casual workers would be employed at harvest time.

Early in the 1930s Mr Fred Field had to retire because of severe rheumatoid arthritis.

Threshing at Moat Farm.

Chapter 7

Chapel & Sunday School

The Little Methodist Chapel lies in the fork of the roads leading to Burford on the left, straight on for Minster Lovell, and to the right, Witney. It has been a chapel since 1853 (Kathy has a copy of the document showing the registration) when a Mr Edward (?) — his other name(s) were not legible — allowed his house to be used for the Primitive Methodists to worship in. The building is just one room and a gallery. In the 1920s and 1930s it was very well attended, with a Sunday school in the morning, a service at three o'clock in the afternoon and another one at six o'clock in the evening.

The Sunday school had outings in the summer sometimes to Evesham, with a picnic by the river, then on to Bishops Cleve where a big farm was turned into a playground, with slides and see-saws and swings. Tea was served in a barn provided by two brothers and a sister—it was well used by many organisations.

The Methodist Chapel.

Sometimes they went on a railway excursion to the seaside—they would walk to the station for trips to Bournemouth or Barry Island.

Their anniversary was always held in early January, with a tea for the children. The older people came along and they would listen to the party pieces that the children had learnt for the occasion. Little Lucy Field was only four-years-old when she sang her first solo, 'Away in a Manger'. Mrs Lohmann was so impressed she gave Lucy a halfcrown, which was a fortune in those days! The cakes and refreshments for the party came from Barnes's and Hardy's—big slab cakes, specially made, lardy and dough cakes, and endless plates of bread and butter—it would all disappear.

Mr Caleb Field was one of the Sunday school teachers, and with two or three others he also played the organ, which was a foot pedal type and had ornamental pipes above.

All the Field family had extraordinary singing voices. Caleb sang tenor, Mr Fred sang bass, his wife sang alto, and their daughters at that time sang soprano, altogether with the rest of the congregation—it was out of this world!

One of the highlights of the year was the carol singing. They

Methodist Chapel Sunday School outing group to Cleve Hill.

started on Christmas eve when they went up the Burford Road, and down to Barnes's shop. Christmas night, from the shop to Pratt's Farm. A large group of singers would gather Christmas morning, and a few of the men walked up to Joslin's Farm.

Brize Norton Methodist were in the Corn Street, Witney Circuit. Corn Street was head of the Primitive Methodists, and High Street for the Welsleyans. In 1932/33 they joined together for the Witney Methodist Circuit.

* * *

The Post Office, and Barnes' shop on the far right.

Abingdon track (joined with Ting Tang lane) a drover's road to Abingdon market.

Chapter 8

Ting Tang Lane
& the Northern End

At the northern end of the village, Hardys was the mainstay of the village community; shop, pub and bakehouse—all fondly called Hardys.

The shop (just like Barnes's and Miss Worley's) provided everything from shoe polish, fresh farm butter (from nearby Sturch's Farm), bacon, cheese, to flour, etcetera, all willingly provided by Miss Hardy and Biney (real name Sebina Akers).

The pub, the real name of which was *The Masons Arms*—so called because of the many stone quarries that provided the Cotswold stone for the stonemasons to work with—were in close vicinity. The quarry men worked with pick and shovel to cut the stone, and they got very dusty and thirsty, hence their need to visit *The Masons Arms*. Biney would serve the beer from a big china jug, carried up from the cellar. We were told that the beer was in perfect condition, drawn from big wooden barrels stored in the cool cellar. No spirits were sold. The floor of the pub was made of Cotswold flagstones, the tables were plain scrub topped wood, with a few benches and a few chairs to sit on; no bar as such, just Biney and the big jug.

The *Bakehouse*, managed and worked by Tom Hardy, was in a stone-built building across the yard, and they provided beautiful bread cooked in a coal-fired oven, but very little in the way of cakes, only dough or farmhouse-style cakes were baked.

A pretty delivery cart, pulled by a horse, took bread and cakes around the village and district. It was the type of vehicle with a fixed hood and ornate carved trim. The delivery man was Alfie Timms, who was so both pleasant and careful.

All in all, Hardys was a very special meeting place for both men and their wives. Village gossip, church and chapel news—all were talked about in either the pub or the shop.

Both shop and bakehouse are now closed. *The Masons Arms* is now a pub and restaurant.

Getting on towards the end of the village was the *Malt House* —a large house facing west. We have forgotten who lived there, although we do know that Tom Hardy was using the barn and outhouses at the rear as a stable for his horse that he used for deliveries. Alfie Timms, who had just started working for Mr Hardy, had the job of taking the horse and breadvan up to the *Malt House* at the end of the day's work.

Alfie had heard the tale of a man named Akers who had hung himself up in the loft above the stable. It was to him just a tale, something that had happened in the past, it did not bother him at all until one dark night with only a flash light he found there was not enough oats for the horse—he would have to go up into the loft. Up he went with the bucket, and as he straightened up after filling the bucket, he felt a weight against his shoulder. In the murky light he saw an object hanging from the beam—he fled down those stairs and out through the door like lightning and then on down the road to the bakery, he gasped out what he had seen! The women could see how white and shaken Alfie was, that it gave them a fright too. The exception was Tommy Hardy, who just roared with laughter and said: "I only hung that 'bag of oats' up this morning to keep it away from the rats." Alfie seemed unconvinced—he had no intention of going back up into the loft!

Kempsford House was, and still is, one of the most imposing houses in Burford Road. Built for Mr Arthur Smith, he was born and lived in Brize Norton village for most of his life. Mr Smith was a very clever business man, who moved to London and seems to have been quite successful there. Mr Packer (Clare's father) found him to be a sincere and genuine customer; any work that could be done in the village was always offered first to Mr Packer, then to other suitable tradespeople.

Kempsford House had a large garden, with one or maybe two

Kempsford House with The Acacias adjoining.

tennis courts. It also had lovely flower borders, attended by Mr Ray James, the gardener. They also employed Frank Ayers in the house for menial tasks, such as cleaning brass—a thing that Frank loved even after he left their employment, having a large collection of brass himself.

During October, in the field opposite *Kempsford House*, a large structure was erected, and most of the village children began to look forward to what was to be the highlight of the Autumn. During the early evening they made their way up to the front of the house to watch the firework display which was part of Michael Smith's birthday celebrations (Michael was the son of Mr and Mrs Arthur Smith). The use of the large structure soon became apparent at the end of the display, even more brilliant fireworks lit up the words: Happy Birthday Michael!

During the schooldays of Clare and Kathy, displays of this size and brilliance were not seen; for this occasion the very large sky rockets and catherine wheels had been brought from London.

After *Kempsford House* and *The Acacias* (where Miss Knight of 'the Bath chair in the church' fame lived - see p.66), were only a few half dug out quarries. In one of the quarries lived Mr and Mrs Jessie Pratley. Jessie helped out at Sturch Farm at haymaking, and at harvest and threshing time. He had a sideline

85

though, pushing a barrow around the village with oddments on, and sometimes bananas—he could then be heard calling out: "any nanas?" Jessie had not had much education and was quite a gypsy type, he wore a red spotted neckerchief, and he had a ruddy complexion. They lived in a caravan in the quarry for some years. Cissi, Jessie's wife, did wonderful cotton lace making, she had all the knowledge in her head, and was unable to pass her experience on because she could not write.

After the dug out quarries came the *Malt House*, here lived Mr Tom Hardy, the baker from *The Masons Arms*. He lived with Miss Scrivens, who was Kathy's and Clare's first teacher at school—also living there was Biney, the one with the jug at *The Masons Arms*. Later Mr Hardy would marry Miss Scrivens but she developed nerve trouble and after a few years went away to to live on the south coast to recuperate. We did not see her again, however.

Behind the *Malt House* were two or three cottages looking towards Burford. In the first lived Mr Tom Timms and his wife, Hilda, and their two daughters, Violet and Betty. Violet was the same age as Clare and Kathy, and was at school with them, other than that we did not know much about the family.

In another of these cottages lived Mr Percy Bellenger and his wife and daughter—we knew nothing about them other than their name.

Right at the bottom lived Mr Fred Giles who earlier had worked in Kathy's grandfather's bakery. Fred lived with his wife, daughter Betty, and sons Sonny, Gordon, Mick and Tony. Mr Giles started up his own business of greengrocery and fish. He delivered around Brize Norton with his horse and covered cart. The green groceries were always very fresh and nicely displayed—he was a welcome addition to the village.

Later, Fred started up a fish and chip shop. This he also delivered around the village—the fish was delicious and he was very popular. Fred sold his cooked fish for only threepence a piece. He also sold chips and the most lovely potato scollops; these were much in demand and were very filling. Later he made more of his greengrocery business, selling from his quarters which was also another stone quarry. Much later he began a delivery business with his son, Mick, and they went round the area in a big van.

'Ting Tang Lane', also known as the 'Green Lane', at the top of the village, was rather out of bounds for both Kathy and Clare when they were small children. On a school nature study walk they were taken by 'Boss' Jones, who explained it was an old Roman road, proven by the fact that if searched for, there were stones laid side by side upright, to make the base of the road. The lane led to the small hamlet of Worsham, where there were just a few remains of a Roman Villa, mainly small tiles and pieces of decorated pavement.

On either side of Ting Tang Lane were stone walls, beautifully created by real craftsmen, not a trace of cement or anything to hold the stones in place. It is quoted that a dry stone waller (as the wall builders were called) could see in each piece of stone that they picked up, a place where to put it. Once picked up it was never laid down but added to the wall. These same walls have stood throughout the Cotswold area for hundreds of years, finished off at the top by toppers laid tightly together so that

Nature Study walk to Worsham with Mr Jones, going up Green Lane (Ting Tang).

they remained firmly in place. The stone was produced by local Cotswold quarries.

'Boss' Jones explained to us as children that the walls themselves contained fossils of sea shells, proving that at some time the area must have been under water.

Ting Tang joined up with another lane, known locally as Abingdon Track. Along these lanes, which together became a drovers' road, were driven sheep gathered from the farms and hillsides to be sold at Abingdon Market—just think of the miles those sheep walked!

Kathy and Clare were fascinated by the masses of wild flowers along both sides of the lane; violets, primroses and in season, cowslips and bluebells grew, and not to be forgotten, Kathy's favourite: the bright pink dog-roses, they filled the air with their sweetness.

The flowers at Worsham end of the lane were quite different to those at the lower end of the village. *Greater Knapweed, Lady's Bedstraw,* and *Common Mallow.* It was the poor quality of the soil which made the difference, possibly the start of the Cotswold hills. It was a most glorious place, and when Kathy and Clare became older, they would venture up here to gather a grand collection for the competition for the best collection of wild flowers, which was held at the village fete.

In Brize Norton village was, and still is, a rich dark brown loam—very fertile and capable of growing good crops of fruit, flowers and vegetables.

At the top of the village, making our way towards Burford we come to a terrace of cottages sideways on to the road, known locally as *Dottom's Row.* Mr Drinkwater had a wooden leg, it seemed to us almost 'magic' that anyone could walk with just a wooden rod for a leg, but he gardened and walked with apparently no particular problems. As he walked the wooden leg went 'clonk' on the road, a sort of 'Dot and Carry One', hence the name 'Dottom'!

He was Sexton at the church (helped by his wife), and the church was always very, very clean, pews all polished, and in

Ivy Villas in August 1952, home of Mercy Joynes.

the winter the old tortoise stove was lit well before service time. Dottom was also the village 'grave digger' under Mr Packer's instructions when occasion demanded.

Dottom Drinkwater's garden was aways very productive, and he always seemed to have apples or vegetables to sell, or give to neighbours.

In the quarry on the opposite side of the road was another garden and some beehives, the honey of which he sold either in jars or in slabs of honeycomb. Clare used to often have a slab of

View from the back of Ivy Villas.
The Barracks on the left and Dottom's Row chimneys just visible over the high wall.

89

Dottom's honey for tea. Dottom was quite a feature in Clare's life, but less so in Kathy's because she lived at the other end of the village.

Adjoining the quarry in Kilkenny Lane, which is a short cut through to the village of Carterton, was also the approach to Kilkenny Farm and *Kilkenny Cottage*. Why Kilkenny? We know not, but it still is a very pretty lane particularly in springtime.

If we continue up the Burford Road we come to a square building known as the 'Lodge'. It was actually the home for two families who worked at Kilkenny Farm. Children from the Lodge attended Brize Norton School, but we never got to know them very well because they were aways moving on, and also so far out of the village. Adjoining was a pleasant and dense wood, and next to this was a small building that was rather unusual. This was the home of Mr George Fitchett and his wife Ada. George was our roadman who cleaned the roads and kept the drains free. We heard how the bungalow had been built by Ada's father, whose name was 'Snobby' Smith. As his name suggests, he was a shoe mender, whose business was in Burford. He made the start on his bungalow by taking down and using the frontage wall of his piece of land. From there he began to look elsewhere for more stone, and as he walked to Burford most days pushing his hand cart, on his way back home he would help himself to some toppers off the roadside walls. These walls are such a characteristic feature of Brize Norton and the sur-rounding villages, bordering the roads and fields, in some places they are as much as six feet high. It is said that he took more of them and in places left gaps spoiling the whole effect of these continual walls. He never finished off the bungalow properly and it always leaned to one side, especially the front door, which caught one's eye when passing. He didn't point the walls either, and the only floor was a dirt one. George and Ada continued living in the bungalow, trying to make it reasonably comfortable, and they lived out the rest of their lives in this sad condition.

A little further up the road on the same side was a completely different bungalow; this was the home of Mr Ray James and his wife. In contrast, theirs always looked so spick and span, nicely painted with a pretty garden in the front, and a real pleasure to look at.

Almost the last pair of cottages in the village in Brize Norton were on the right hand side. From one of them came a girl named Eileen James, who was the same age as Kathy and Clare. Eileen walked to school and back in all weathers, a distance of nearly two miles, to attend lessons. This was a very long way for a young girl to walk. These cottages again linked with Kilkenny Farm, and were called by the charming name of *Lingermans*, and this was the very end of the village as Clare and Kathy knew it.

* * *

Brize Norton Village Forge was adequate in the early days of the Blacksmith,
but not in the later days of local rural engineer, John Cambray (pictured here),
whose engineering business quickly outgrew these premises.

BRIZE NORTON, OXON,

Xmas 1927

Copy sent to M[r] Barnes

Dr. to F. W. TIMMS,
Slater, Plasterer, &c.

ALL KINDS OF BUILDING WORK EXECUTED.

Date	Description	£	s	d
May 14 1923	For 58 hrs Labour & Buss Adamant and Materials for White Washing, Repairing Plaster, and for Blue Slates and Nails to Repairs to Roof at the shop for Mr J Barnes	3	15	6
May 19th '23	For Labours and Materials to White-Washing, Distempering and Papering Kitchen etc, at the Poplars for Mr W Barnes	2	14	6
Nov 29th '23	For Repairs to Old Bakehouse Roof		7	6
April 30th 24	Whitewashing and Repairing Furnace at Mr J Barnes.	1	13	6
May 3rd '24	Repairing Wall and Plaster in Offal Room at Mr J Barnes	1	12	0
Oct 2nd 25	For Labour Lime Cement and Iron Grating for Drain, for fixing New Oven Building Walls and Converting Cart Shed into New Bakehouse for Mr W Barnes	23	8	0
Oct 13 & 24 and Mar 5th/25	For Labour and Blue Slates and Nails and Cement to Repairs to Old Bakehouse and Other Roofs at the Shop. Cleaning Out Guttering etc, for Mr J Barnes.	1	14	6
		35	5	6

Village builder's bill made out Xmas 1927.

How far is it to Lingermans?
As the crow flies
From Diddley Corner, going all up through Brize

Take it slowly, stop on the way,
Visit old friends, many have passed away

There's Thatchers and Hummy, Miss Worley too,
Lots more in this book, especially for you

When we get to Lingermans, we turn round you see,
And go back down to Dottom's,
And get honey for tea!

The 'Axe' Pub. (Painting and verse by Kathy Timms).

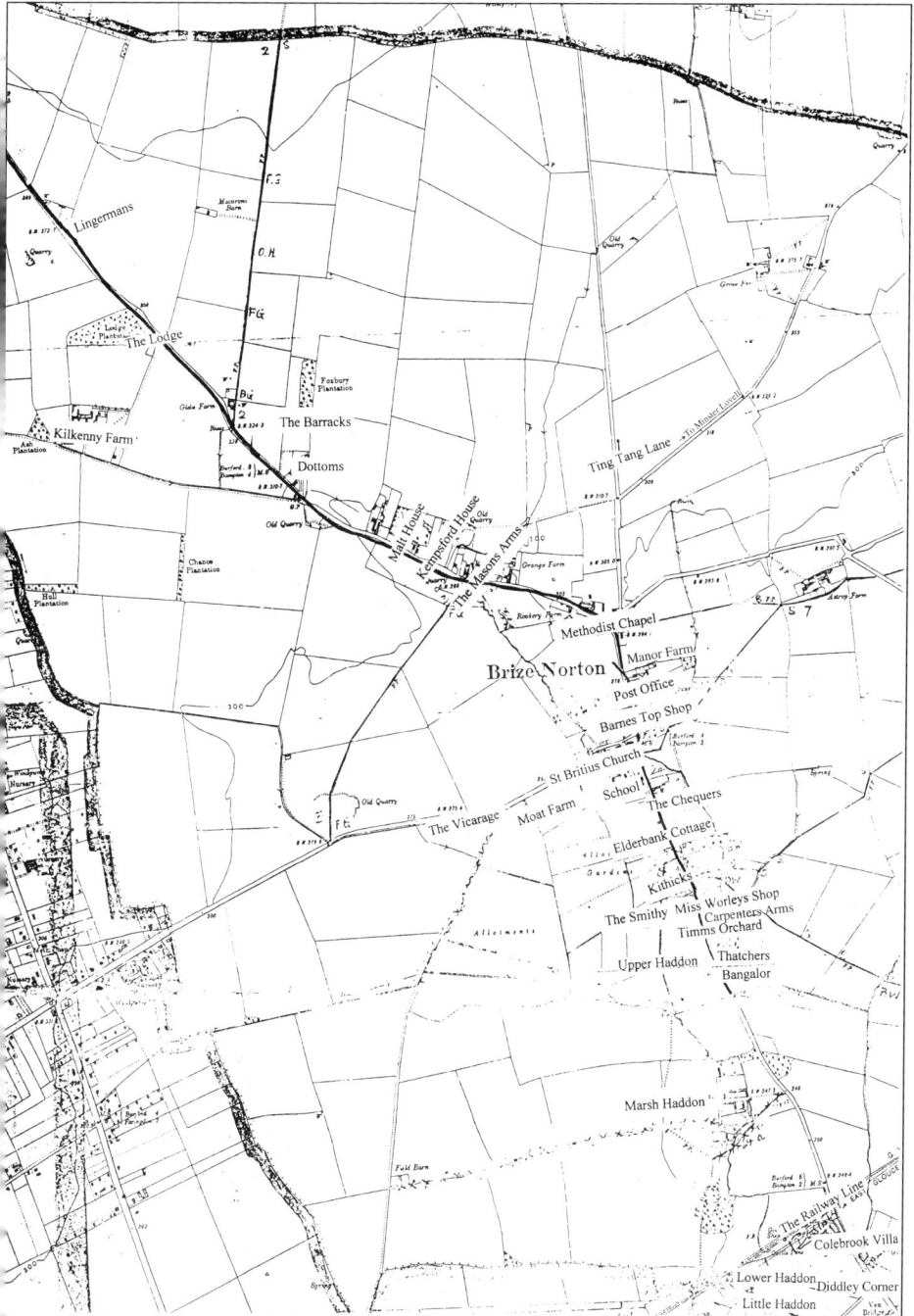

PHOTO IDENTIFICATION

Scandinavian Dancers photo page 63
Back row: Mr Jones (head), Dora Drinkwater, George Wheeler, Harry Humphries, Alec Badger, Arthur Timms, Edie Archer, Mrs Jones (wife of head).
Seated: Marie Packer, Janet Timms, Phyllis Badger, Lucy Field.
On ground: Elsie Ashby, Vera Faulkner, Peggie Ashby.

Girls Cookery Class photo page 77
Back row: Iris Preston, Katherine Taylor, Phyllis Badger, Eva Field.
Front row: Vera Faulkner, May Parker, Mary Wilkins, Marjorie Jones, Annie Siford, Violet Hayward.

Methodist Chapel Sunday School Outing photo page 80
Back row: Bill Upstone, Eva Field, Lucy Field, Mr Bert Bye, Caleb Field.
Second row: Pearl Timms, Bertha James, Mary Winfield, Louise Bellenger, unknown?
Sitting: Fred Faulkner, Gordon Timms, Sonny James, Sidney Timms, Joe Faulkner.
Front sitting: John Bellenger, Ruth Bellenger, Jimmy Barnes.

Nature Study Walk Group photo page 87
Those identified: Alec Badger, Fred Mills, Vera Faulkner, Eileen Hedges, John Preston, Marie Packer, John Coggins, Mr Jones (head), Elsie Ashby, Dora Drinkwater, Frank Handford, Bill Upstone.